Fifth Edition

Study Guide and Workbook to accompany

FINANCIAL INSTITUTIONS, INVESTMENTS, and MANAGEMENT: An Introduction

Herbert B. Mayo
Trenton State College

The Dryden Press
Harcourt Brace College Publishers

Fort Worth · Philadelphia · San Diego · New York · Orlando · Austin · San Antonio
Toronto · Montreal · London · Sydney · Tokyo

Address for Editorial Correspondence
The Dryden Press, 301 Commerce Street, Suite 3700, Fort Worth, TX 76102

Address for Orders
The Dryden Press, 6277 Sea Harbor Drive, Orlando, FL 32887
1-800-782-4479, or 1-800-433-0001 (in Florida)

ISBN: 0-03-098652-4

Printed in the United States of America

4 5 6 7 8 9 0 1 2 3   0 2 3   9 8 7 6 5 4 3 2 1

The Dryden Press
Harcourt Brace College Publishers

TABLE OF CONTENTS

PREFACE

Financial Institutions, Investments, and Management, fifth edition, is designed to introduce you to financial institutions, investments, and financial management. Such an introduction is potentially useful to all students whether they are majoring in finance or other fields. If you are a finance major, this introduction will serve as a foundation upon which to build. For non-finance majors this introduction will increase your ability to communicate within the business community. In addition, finance is also part of your everyday private world. Knowledge of financial institutions, investments, and financial management can only increase your ability to function in modern society.

Several features of the text should help you learn the material. Each chapter begins with learning objectives. This aid is reinforced by the introductory paragraphs and the summary at the end of the chapter. Terms are defined in the margin as they appear in the text. I have had students tell me that they began the chapter by reading the summaries first and that this strategy gives them a good indication of the content of the chapter. However, you must realize that learning aids are of little use if you superficially read the text material. There is no substitute for a thorough, concentrated reading of each paragraph.

This workbook/study guide will help you learn the material. However, it is not meant to be a substitute for the text. This material is only a supplementary aid to help you understand financial concepts and institutions. First, an outline of the chapter is presented. This is followed by a chapter summary. Next many of the equations presented in the chapter are reproduced and illustrated. There are simple problems for you to solve, and you may test your knowledge by means of various techniques: fill-in-the-blanks, true-false statements, and multiple choice questions. Answers to fill-in-the-blanks and the problems follow the multiple choice questions. The answers to the true-false statements and multiple choice questions are presented in tables at the end of this workbook.

Chapter 1
INTRODUCTION TO FINANCE

I. Key Financial Concepts
   A. Sources of finance: debt and equity
   B. Risk and return
      1. Anticipated return justifies investments
      2. Uncertainty of the return (risk)
      3. Diversifiable risk: business and financial risk
      4. Non-diversifiable risk
         a. Market risk
         b. Interest rate risk
         c. Reinvestment rate risk
         d. Purchasing power risk
         e. Exchange rate risk

II. Valuation
   A. Process for determining what something is worth
   B. Maximization of value as the goal of management

III. Plan of the Text
   A. Financial institutions
   B. Investments
   C. Corporate finance
   D. Finance careers
   E. Computer applications

SUMMARY

The study of financial institutions, investments, and corporate finance is important to both individuals and financial managers. Money, credit, the stock market, the banking system, pension plans, foreign exchange, and other financial institutions are part of our everyday lives.

Firms (and individuals and governments) must have assets in order to operate. All assets must be financed. This financing either comes from the owners (e.g., stockholders in the case of corporations) or from creditors (e.g., commercial banks and other creditors such as bondholders). A balance sheet enumerates these assets, liabilities, and equity.

Investments are made because investors anticipate a return through income or price appreciation. Since the future is not certain, investments involve risk. The sources of risk include the nature of the business and how the operation was financed (i.e., business risk and financial risk, respectively). Financial risk results from using debt financing which may increase the owners' return on their investment in the firm. These sources of risk may be reduced through the construction of diversified portfolios.

Other sources of risk include (1) the tendency for security prices to fluctuate (market risk), (2) fluctuations in interest rates which causes security prices to change, (3) reinvestment rate risk, (4) loss of purchasing power from inflation, and (4) fluctuations in exchange rates (that is, fluctuations in the prices of foreign currencies). These sources of risk are not reduced through the construction of diversified portfolios.

Valuation is the process of determining the present value of future cash flows. In finance, the goal of management is specified as the maximization of the value of the firm. Management should make those decisions which increase the value of the firm.

TRUE/FALSE

T F 1. In finance the goal of management is the maximization of sales and profits.

T F 2. How a firm finances its operation is the source of financial risk.

T F 3. Business risk depends on the size of the firm.

T F 4. Successful business administration does not require successful financial administration.

T F 5. The tendency for security prices to fluctuate is the source of exchange rate risk.

T F 6. The use of borrowed funds is a source of business risk.

T F 7. If interest rates decline, that is a source of reinvestment rate risk.

T F 8. The process of determining what future payments are currently worth is called valuation.

T F 9. Assets minus equity equals liabilities.

T F 10. The sum of liabilities and equity must equal total assets.

MULTIPLE CHOICE

1. Finance combines concepts from
    a. economics and marketing
    b. management and economics
    c. accounting and management
    d. accounting and economics

2. Which of the following is excluded from a balance sheet?
   a. assets
   b. liabilities
   c. equity
   d. revenues

3. Business risk refers to the risk associated with
   a. how a firm is financed
   b. the firm's operations
   c. fluctuations in exchange rates
   d. financial forecasting

4. In finance, the financial manager's goal is maximization of
   a. profits
   b. earnings
   c. the firm's value
   d. sales

5. Exchange rate risk refers to the risk associated with fluctuating
   a. security prices
   b. interest rates
   c. currency prices
   d. commodity prices

6. Debt financing may
   a. increase the firm's business risk
   b. increase the return achieved by the firm's owners
      (its equity)
   c. decrease the firm's market risk
   d. decrease the firm's interest rate risk

7. Valuation is
   a. the construction of a balance sheet
   b. the determination of the historical cost of an asset
   c. discounting future cash flows
   d. liquidating a firm

Chapter 2

THE CREATION OF FINANCIAL ASSETS

I. The Role of Money
   A. Money: anything that is generally acceptable as a means of payment
   B. Forms of money: currency, coins, and demand deposits
   C. The functions of money:
      1. Medium of exchange
      2. Store of value
      3. Unit of account
      4. Standard of deferred payment
   D. The power to create money rests with the Federal Reserve
   E. The value of money: what it purchases
   F. Definitions (measures) of the money supply: M-1 and M-2

II. The Role of Interest Rates
   A. Interest: the cost of credit
   B. The variety of debt
   C. Term structure of yields: generally short-term debt costs less than long-term debt

III. The Transfer of Funds to Business
   A. The direct transfer of savings to firms
   B. The indirect transfer (i.e., the role of financial intermediaries)

IV. The Issuing and Selling of New Securities
   A. The role of the investment banker
   B. The mechanics of underwriting
   C. Types of agreements: best efforts and underwriting
   D. Marketing new securities
   E. Volatility of the new issue market
   F. Shelf-registrations
   G. Venture capitalists

SUMMARY

Money is anything that is generally accepted for payment. Money primarily serves as a medium of exchange. It may be held in checking accounts (which may or may not pay interest) as a store of value, and it also serves as a unit of account and a standard of deferred payments.

The Constitution gives Congress the power to create money. Congress uses the United States Treasury to distribute money. The Federal Reserve is the nation's central bank and was created by Congress to regulate and control the supply of money.

The money supply (M-1) is narrowly defined as all coins and currency in circulation plus all deposits in banks on which checks may be drawn. Broader definitions of the money supply (such as M-2) add savings deposits and small denomination time deposits to M-1.

An interest rate is the price paid for the use of money. There are many types of debt instruments with specific features such as the maturity date. Generally, the longer the term of the debt, the greater is the interest rate. This relationship between yields and the term is shown by a yield curve.

Funds may be transferred to borrowers directly when individual savers purchase newly issued securities or invest in sole proprietorships and partnerships. Funds may be transferred indirectly from savers to borrowers through financial intermediaries such as a commercial bank.

Besides retaining earnings and borrowing from a financial intermediary, a firm acquires funds by issuing new securities. The usual procedure is for the firm to secure the services of an investment banker to market the new issue.

There are two types of agreements with investment bankers for the issue of new securities: a best efforts offering or an underwriting of the entire issue by the investment bankers. An underwriting means that the investment bankers buy the securities and subsequently resell them. An underwriting guarantees the issuing firm a specified amount of money and transfers the risk of selling the securities to the investment bankers.

The sale of new securities to the general public requires that the securities be registered with the Securities and Exchange Commission (SEC). New securities may also be privately placed with a financial institution such as an insurance company or with a venture capital firm that specializes in investing in small, emerging firms.

FILL IN THE BLANKS

1. The composition of M-1 includes _____, _____, and _____.

2. The composition of M-2 includes _____, _____, _____, and _____.

3. The four functions (roles) of money are _____.

4. The payment for the use of money is called _____.

5. The value of money is its _____.

6. A financial intermediary creates a _____ on itself.

7. The structure of yields is indicated by a _____.

8. To sell a new issue of securities, many firms use the services of _____.

9. To facilitate selling a new issue of securities, the originating investment banker forms a _____.

10. Before a new issue of securities may be sold to the general public, the securities must be _____ with the _____.

11. In a best efforts sale of securities, the risk of selling rests with _____.

12. The document giving pertinent information concerning a new issue of securities is the _____.

13. Small, emerging firms may raise money by selling securities to a _____.

TRUE/FALSE

T F 1. A general decline in prices also decreases the value of money.

T F 2. Money is a better store of value than other assets because it earns interest.

T F 3. Only paper and metal can perform the function of money.

T F 4. Stocks and bonds are a substitute for money as a store of value.

T F 5. What serves for money in France may not be money in another country.

T F 6. The U. S. Treasury creates most of the nation's money.

T F 7. When individuals deposit cash in a demand deposit, the money supply is not affected.

T F 8. M-1 includes savings accounts in commercial banks.

T F 9. A financial intermediary creates claims on itself, when it accepts depositors' funds.

T F 10. If a firm issues securities that are sold to the general public, savings are directly transferred to the firm.

T F 11. M-2 excludes NOW accounts in savings banks.

T F 12. A financial intermediary stands between the ultimate borrowers and lenders and converts a claim on the lender to one that is acceptable to the borrower.

T F 13. If a company went public at $10 per share and the shares immediately upon reaching the public sell for $13, the $3 windfall gain goes to the underwriter.

T F 14. If an investment banker makes a best efforts agreement to sell 200,000 shares at $4 a share, the investment banker must sell the 200,000 shares.

T F 15. A prospectus gives estimates of a firm's prospective earnings for five years.

T F 16. The larger the dollar value of an underwriting, the smaller is the fee as a percentage of the offer price.

T F 17. In an underwriting the managing house forms the syndicate.

T F 18. If an issue of securities is overpriced, the underwriters may let the price fall to sell the securities.

T F 19. The purchasing of a new issue of stock is different than buying stock on the NYSE because in the former funds flow to the firm while in the latter the funds flow to the individual selling the shares.

T F 20. The SEC establishes a price for a new issue of securities.

T F 21. A major function of the NYSE is to facilitate the transfer of funds between investors and firms.

MULTIPLE CHOICE

1. The term structure of interest rates indicates the
    a. relationship between risk and yields
    b. relationship between the time to maturity and yields
    c. the difference between borrowing and lending
    d. the difference between the yield on short-term and long-term debt

2. A financial intermediary transfers
    a. savings to households
    b. savings to borrowers
    c. stocks to brokers
    d. new stock issues to buyers

3. The value of money
   a. rises as prices rise
   b. is the cost of borrowing
   c. declines as prices increase
   d. depends on gold

4. Money serves as
   a. a substitute for equity
   b. a precaution against inflation
   c. a medium of exchange
   d. a risk free liability

5. An asset is liquid if it is easily
   a. converted into cash
   b. marketed
   c. converted into cash without loss
   d. sold

6. M-2 includes
   1. demand deposits
   2. savings accounts
   3. negotiable small certificates of deposit
      a. 1 and 2
      b. 2 and 3
      c. 1 and 3
      d. all three

7. An investment banker
   1. is usually not a banker
   2. is frequently a division of a brokerage firm
   3. serves as a middleman between financial intermediaries
      and firms issuing new securities
      a. 1 and 2
      b. 1 and 3
      c. 2 and 3
      d. only 3

8. Which of the following is not part of the underwriting process?
   a. the syndicate
   b. the originating house
   c. the prospectus
   d. the secondary market

9. A venture capitalist
   a. buys existing securities
   b. is a source of funds for large firms
   c. buys securities issued by small, emerging firms
   d. must register the securities it purchases with the SEC

10. If the initial offer price is too low,
    1. supply will exceed demand
    2. demand will exceed supply
    3. the price of the security will rise
    4. the price of the security will decline
       a. 1 and 3
       b. 1 and 4
       c. 2 and 3
       d. 2 and 4

11. An investment banker is not a financial intermediary because
    a. it does not transfer money from investors to firms
    b. it does not create claims on itself
    c. it does facilitate the transfer of funds
    d. it creates claims on itself

ANSWERS TO FILL IN THE BLANKS

1. coins, currency, and demand deposits (including NOW accounts)

2. coins, currency, demand deposits, savings accounts, and small time deposits

3. medium of exchange, store of value, standard of deferred payments, unit of account

4. interest

5. purchasing power

6. claim

7. yield curve

8. investment banker

9. syndicate

10. registered, SEC

11. firm issuing the securities

12. prospectus

13. venture capitalist

Chapter 3
FINANCIAL INTERMEDIARIES

I. The Variety of Financial Intermediaries
  A. Trend to blur distinctions among financial intermediaries
  B. Advantages of financial intermediaries
    1. To borrowers
    2. To savers
    3. To the financial intermediary
    4. To the economy

II. Commercial banks
  A. A Commercial bank's balance sheet
    1. Loans and tax-exempt securities
    2. Demand deposits
    3. Savings accounts and certificates of deposit
    4. Equity
  B. A Commercial bank's earnings
    1. Revenues and expenses
    2. Small profit margin
    3. Return earned for stockholders
    4. Impact of financial leverage

III. Regulation of Commercial Banks
  A. Protection for depositors from bank failure
  B. Sources of regulation: federal and state
  C. Reserve requirements against deposit liabilities
  D. Excess reserves: total reserves minus required reserves
  E. Deposit insurance: FDIC
  F. Trends in regulation

IV. Thrift Institutions
  A. Mutual savings banks
  B. Savings and loan associations (S&Ls)

V. Life Insurance Companies

VI. Pension Plans

VII. Investment Companies: Money Market Mutual Funds

VIII. Competition for Funds

IX. The Savings and Loan Debacle
  A. The causes of S&L failures
  B. The creation of the Resolution Trust Corporation
  C. Large losses sustained by taxpayers

SUMMARY

There are many financial intermediaries. Differences among them are diminishing as the result of the deregulation of the banking system.

Financial intermediation is the transfer through an intermediary of savings to borrowers. There are advantages to all concerned. For the borrower, financial intermediaries pool the funds of many savers; for the saver, the process provides interest income and safety of principal. For the intermediary, the process provides a potential source of profits. The economy also benefits as the process expands the nation's level of output and employment.

The most important financial intermediary is the commercial banking system. Through commercial banks funds are transferred from lenders to borrowers. Demand deposits in commercial banks constitute a substantial part of the nation's money supply (M-1 and M-2).

The deposits of customers constitute most of a commercial bank's liabilities. Loans constitute most of its assets. Because the liabilities of a bank far outweigh its equity, the bank is considered to be highly financially leveraged.

Commercial banks must hold reserves against their deposit liabilities. Reserve requirements are set by the Federal Reserve. Any funds held in excess of the required reserves may be lent.

Savings and loan associations and mutual savings banks are primarily depositories for savers' funds. These "thrift" institutions primarily (but not exclusively) invest in mortgage loans. Life insurance companies invest in a variety of assets, but about 2/3rds of their investments are mortgage loans and corporate securities. Pension plans are designed to invest funds now to finance the individual's retirement. These plans may acquire existing securities (such as corporate stock traded on the New York Stock Exchange) and newly issued debt instruments. When these funds purchase existing securities, they are not acting as a financial intermediary because funds are transferred from the fund to the seller of the securities and not to the issuer of the securities.

Money market mutual funds developed in response to increased short-term interest rates. These funds invest primarily in short-term financial assets such as Treasury bills. They compete vigorously with the other financial intermediaries for the funds. This competition may affect segments of the economy if financial intermediaries have specialized portfolios. Flows into and out of these intermediaries affect their ability to grant loans and hence affect the supply of credit in that particular segment of the economy.

The late 1980s saw the failure of many financial intermediaries, especially savings and loan associations. Several causes of these failures include excessive risky loans made by the associations, the high interest paid for deposits, and mismanagement. Federally insured depositors, however, did not sustain losses even though the losses exceeded the capacity of FSLIC to cover the insured deposits. Instead the losses were transferred to taxpayers as the federal government changed the regulatory environment and upheld the insuring of deposits. This change in the regulatory environment lead to the creation of the Office of Thrift Supervision and the Resolution Trust Corporation to oversee the assets of failed thrifts and to liquidate (sell) their assets.

FILL IN THE BLANKS

1. One purpose of the regulation of commercial banks is to protect _____.

2. Commercial banks stress acquiring assets that are _____ and _____.

3. The primary assets of commercial banks include _____ and _____.

4. Deposits in commercial banks may be insured by _____.

5. Cash deposited in commercial banks increases their _____ reserves.

6. The reserve requirement for savings accounts is _____ than the requirement for demand deposits.

7. The supervisory power over the banking system rests with the _____.

8. The primary asset of savings and loan associations is _____.

9. The largest financial intermediary in terms of total assets is _____.

10. Deposits in savings and loan associations are insured by _____.

11. During the early 1980s the largest growing financial intermediary was _____.

12. The Financial Reform, Recovery, and Enforcement Act gave the power to size failed savings and loans to the _____.

13. A flow of funds from money market mutual funds to savings and loan associations will tend to _____ the supply of mortgage funds.

14. The deregulation of the banking system has tended to _____ competition among financial intermediaries.

TRUE/FALSE

T F 1. The Federal Reserve has the power to fix the minimum rate of interest that commercial banks may pay on savings accounts.

T F 2. The Federal Reserve establishes the minimum rate of interest that commercial banks charge borrowers.

T F 3. The Monetary Control Act of 1980 gave the regulatory power over commercial banks to the Resolution Trust Corporation.

T F 4. The primary purpose of bank regulation is to protect the owners of commercial banks.

T F 5. Prior to the establishment of FDIC, losses from bank failures were limited to the bank's stockholders.

T F 6. Commercial banks primarily make profits by borrowing from corporations and making mortgage loans.

T F 7. Commercial banks' primary source of profits is their investments in municipal bonds.

T F 8. Commercial banks earn a small amount on their assets (i.e., $.01 on $1.00).

T F 9. A shift of funds from savings accounts to checking accounts will increase banks' excess reserves.

T F 10. The most important financial intermediary is the pension plan.

T F 11. By facilitating the transfer of savings into investments, financial intermediaries increase the level of economic activity.

T F 12. Life insurance companies do not acquire corporate stocks but do hold corporate bonds.

T F 13. Money market mutual funds invest in long-term (i.e., more than one year) securities.

T F 14. Money market mutual funds grew rapidly after their inception and prior to the deregulation of the banking system.

T F 15. Deregulation of the banking system has increased competition among the various financial intermediaries.

T F 16. FDIC insures deposits in savings and loan associations.

T F 17. Many savings and loan associations violate a major principle of finance in that they borrow short and lend long.

T F 18. The primary losers from the failure of savings and loan associations are U.S. taxpayers.

T F 19. The Resolution Trust Corporation has the power to seize (take over) a savings and loan and sell its assets.

T F 20. The Office of Thrift Supervision insures pension plans.

MULTIPLE CHOICE

1. Which of the following is not a financial intermediary?
   a. commercial banks
   b. American Stock Exchange
   c. savings and loan associations
   d. money market mutual fund

2. The typical commercial bank's liabilities include
   a. inventory
   b. buildings
   c. deposits
   d. stock

3. The typical commercial bank's assets include
   1. consumer loans
   2. reserves
   3. commercial loans
      a. 1 and 2
      b. 1 and 3
      c. 2 and 3
      d. 1, 2, and 3

4. The reserves of commercial banks must be held against
   a. the bank's equity
   b. losses
   c. savings deposits
   d. commercial loans

5. Since commercial banks have a large amount of debt outstanding,
   a. they are highly financially leveraged
   b. they earn very little for their stockholders
   c. they pay high interest rates on deposits
   d. they pay dividends to their stockholders

6. If a bank is fully loaned up,
   a. it has excess reserves
   b. it has the maximum allowed number of deposits
   c. it has no excess reserves
   d. it has no required reserves

7. If $100 cash is deposited in a checking account,
   a. excess reserves are increased by $100
   b. required reserves are increased by $100
   c. total reserves are increased by $100
   d. reserves are not affected

8. The primary assets of savings and loan associations are
   a. corporate bonds
   b. corporate stocks
   c. mortgage loans
   d. short-term government securities

9. A pension plan that purchases existing common stock is
   1. an example of a financial intermediary
   2. not an example of a financial intermediary
   3. participating in the primary market
   4. participating in the secondary market
      a. 1 and 3
      b. 1 and 4
      c. 2 and 3
      d. 2 and 4

10. Money market mutual funds
    a. invest in long-term assets
    b. invest only in short-term assets
    c. make mortgage loans
    d. issue savings accounts

11. The failure of many savings and loan associations may be
    partially attributed to
    a. excessive holdings of government securities
    b. selling savings accounts
    c. excessive risky loans
    d. issuing junk bonds

12. Life insurance companies
    a. have federally insured life insurance policies
    b. stress short-term, liquid assets
    c. compete with commercial banks for deposits
    d. can estimate when policies will require payments

ANSWERS TO FILL IN THE BLANKS

1. depositors

2. safe (short-term), liquid

3. commercial loans, government securities (Treasury bills)

4. Federal Deposit Insurance Corporation (FDIC)

5. total (also required and excess reserves)

6. less

7. Federal Reserve

8. mortgage loans

9. commercial banking system

10. Savings Association Insurance Fund (SAIF)

11. money market mutual funds

12. Resolution Trust Corporation (RTC)

13. increase

14. increase

Chapter 4
THE FEDERAL RESERVE AND THE SUPPLY AND COST OF CREDIT

I. The Role of the Federal Reserve System
   A. Goals of monetary policy: stable prices, full
      employment, and economic growth
   B. The Federal Reserve's balance sheet
     1. Gold certificates
     2. Federal government debt
     3. Cash items in process -- the float
     4. Loans to banks
     5. Federal Reserve notes
     6. Reserves of banks (and supervisory powers)
   C. Structure of the Federal Reserve
     1. Board of Governors
     2. District banks
     3. Member banks
     4. Federal Open Market Committee

II. The Expansion of Money and Credit
   A. Cash deposits create new excess reserves
   B. Excess reserves are loaned and new deposits are created
   C. The second bank creates new loans
   D. The complete multiple expansion
   E. Assumptions necessary for the multiple expansion
   F. Cash withdrawals
     1. Multiple contraction
     2. Sources of reserves
     3. Federal funds market
     4. Borrowing from the Federal Reserve

III. Tools of Monetary Policy
   A. Discount rate: cost of borrowing from the Fed
   B. Reserve requirements for deposit liabilities
   C. Open market operations: the buying and selling of
      government securities by the Fed

IV. Fiscal Policy and Financing the Federal Government's
   Deficits
   A. Treasury borrows from the general public
   B. Treasury borrows from the banks
   C. Treasury borrows from the Federal Reserve

V. Impact of Inflationary Economic Environment on Credit Markets
   A. Inflation and the Consumer Price Index
   B. Real rate of interest
   C. Deflation and recession

VI. Impact of Monetary and Fiscal Policy on the Firm
   A. Impact on cost of credit
   B. Impact on earnings

SUMMARY

The Federal Reserve is the nation's central bank. It is owned by the member banks, and all national banks must join the Federal Reserve system.

The purpose of the Federal Reserve is to control the supply of money to promote stable prices, high employment, and economic growth. The federal government also pursues the same economic goals, though at times the Federal Reserve seems at odds with the federal government in pursuing these goals.

The Fed controls the supply of money and credit through its impact on the reserves of commercial banks. The fractional reserve banking system results in multiple expansions in the money supply when reserves are put into the banking system. When cash is deposited in a bank, the cash becomes part of the bank's reserves. While a portion of the reserves are required against the bank's deposit liabilities, the majority are excess reserves which the bank may lend.

When the funds are loaned, borrowers usually redeposit the money back into the banking system. These funds are, in turn, lent to other borrowers. This continual depositing-borrowing cycle results in a multiple expansion of the supply of money and credit. This expansion in credit provides funds needed by individuals, businesses, and government. The removal of reserves has the opposite effect and produces a multiple contraction in the money supply.

Commercial banks that lack sufficient reserves to meet their reserves requirement may borrow them from other banks. If a commercial bank has excess reserves (i.e., is not fully loaned up), it may lend these excess reserves to other banks through the federal funds market.

Monetary policy is accomplished through the reserve requirements for banks' deposit liabilities, the discount rate, and open market operations (the buying and selling of government securities by the Federal Reserve.) By manipulating the reserves of banks, the Federal Reserve is able to alter banks' capacity to lend and hence to alter the supply of money in the economy.

When the Open Market Committee judges that an "easy" monetary policy is desirable, the Federal Reserve purchases securities, which makes more funds (i.e., reserves) available for lending. When a "tight" monetary policy is considered appropriate, the Federal Reserve sells securities, which reduces the lending capacity (i.e., reserves) of banks.

Fiscal policy is government taxation, spending, and debt management. When expenditures exceed revenues and the federal government is running a deficit, borrowing is necessitated. The government can borrow funds from the general public, the banking system, or the Federal Reserve. Borrowing through the Federal Reserve is the most inflationary of the three sources because such borrowings (and the subsequent spending of the funds) increase the supply of money and the reserves of the banking system.

Inflation is a general increase in prices and is measured by the Consumer Price Index (CPI). While prices have risen during the last twenty years, the rate of increase has varied from year to year.

Expectation of inflation alters economic behavior. It encourages borrowing and spending to acquire goods before their prices rise. This increased demand for funds plus a tighter monetary policy designed to decrease inflationary pressure increases the nominal rate of interest. The real rate of interest (the nominal rate minus the rate of inflation) may become negative if the rate of inflation rises sufficiently.

Recession is a period of falling employment and output. Deflation is a period of declining prices. Reducing the rate of inflation may temporarily result in higher levels of unemployment.

Monetary and fiscal policy affect the firm through their impact on earnings and the cost of capital necessary to make investments.

SUMMARY OF EQUATIONS

Change in money or credit:

(4.1)   change in money supply   = $\dfrac{\text{change in excess reserves}}{\text{reserve requirement}}$
            (or credit)

Example:

Reserve requirement   10%
New cash deposit (in a checking account) $1,000
New excess reserves: $1,000 - (.1)(1,000) = $900
Change in money supply:

(4.1) $900/.1   = $9,000

Note that the process works in reverse so that if cash is withdrawn from the banking system, the money supply will contract. In the previous example, a $1,000 withdrawal will lead to a $9,000 contraction in the money supply if reserves are not restored to the banking system.

FILL IN THE BLANKS

1. The buying and selling of government securities by the Federal Reserve is called _____.

2. If the Federal Reserve seeks to expand the supply of money and credit, it _____ securities.

3. If the Federal Reserve seeks to reduce commercial banks' reserves, it _____ securities.

4. The interest rate charged banks when they borrow reserves from the Federal Reserve is the _____.

5. The Federal Reserve is owned by the _____.

6. The control of the Federal Reserve rests with the _____.

7. The most important assets of the Federal Reserve include _____ and _____.

8. If the float decreases, banks' reserves _____.

9. The Board of Governors has a voting _____ on the _____.

10. If the reserve requirements are increased, the maximum possible expansion in credit is _____.

11. A bank may borrow reserves from other banks in the _____ _____.

12. If the proportion of the money supply held in cash is increased, the maximum possible expansion in money is _____.

13. If the Federal Reserve buys government securities from the public, the money supply is _____.

14. If the federal government's tax receipts are less than its expenditures, it is running a _____.

15. If the federal government borrows from the public to finance a deficit, the money supply is _____.

16. Inflation is a _____ increase in _____.

17. Inflation may be measured by the _____.

18. A period of rising unemployment and a reduction in output is a _____.

19. Expectations of increased inflation encourage _____ but discourage _____.

20. The real rate of interest is the difference between _____ and _____.

21. A period of declining price is called a _____.

QUESTIONS/PROBLEMS

1. What is the change in required reserves and excess reserves caused by the following transactions? The reserve requirements are 20 percent for checking accounts and 10 percent for savings accounts.

   a. $100 cash is deposited in a checking account.

      required reserves   _____
      excess reserves   _____

   b. $100 cash is deposited in a savings account.

      required reserves   _____
      excess reserves   _____

   c. $100 is transferred from a checking account into a savings account.

      required reserves   _____
      excess reserves   _____

   d. $100 cash is withdrawn from a checking account.

      required reserves   _____
      excess reserves   _____

   e. A commercial bank borrows $100 from another bank.

      required reserves   _____
      excess reserves   _____

   f. A corporation borrows $100 from a commercial bank.

      required reserves   _____
      excess reserves   _____

2. What is the effect on (1) demand deposits, (2) required reserves, and (3) excess reserves of commercial banks given the following transactions?

a. As a result of higher short-term interest rates, businesses shift funds from checking accounts to negotiable certificates of deposit.

demand deposits   _____
required reserves   _____
excess reserves   _____

b. After the Christmas holiday season, the public reduces its holdings of cash.

demand deposits   _____
required reserves _____
excess reserves   _____

c. Bank A borrows from Bank B in the federal funds market.

demand deposits   _____
required reserves _____
excess reserves   _____

d. The Federal Reserve lowers the reserve requirement on checking accounts.

demand deposits   _____
required reserves _____
excess reserves   _____

e. The Federal Reserve raises the discount rate but since short-term interest rates have also risen, commercial banks do not reduce their borrowings from the Federal Reserve.

demand deposits   _____
required reserves _____
excess reserves   _____

f. The Federal Reserve sells securities that are purchased by general public.

demand deposits   _____
required reserves _____
excess reserves   _____

g. The Treasury sells a new issue of bonds that are purchased by commercial banks. The Treasury deposits the proceeds of the sale in the banks.

demand deposits   _____
required reserves   _____
excess reserves   _____

h. The Treasury runs a surplus and holds the funds in its account at the Federal Reserve.

demand deposits   _____
required reserves   _____
excess reserves   _____

TRUE/FALSE

T F 1. When the Federal Reserve buys government securities, its liabilities are decreased.

T F 2. The Federal Reserve is independent of the U.S. Treasury and is owned by commercial banks.

T F 3. The Federal Open Market Committee is appointed by the President of the United States.

T F 4. If there were no excess reserves in the commercial banking system, new cash deposits of $2 billion increase excess reserves by $2 billion.

T F 5. The cashing of a check does not affect commercial banks' reserves.

T F 6. National banks deposit their reserves in the Federal Reserve while state banks keep their reserves in their vaults.

T F 7. National banks must join the Federal Reserve.

T F 8. Since the reserves of commercial banks earn interest, there is an incentive to hold excess reserves.

T F 9. Open market operations is a more flexible tool of monetary policy than the discount rate.

T F 10. The reserve requirement is seldom changed to affect commercial bank lending.

T F 11. If there are excess reserves in the banking system and the Federal Reserve raises the reserve requirement, the supply of money decreases.

T F 12. Commercial banks hold short-term assets such as Treasury bills because they are safe, self-liquidating investments.

T F 13. Commercial banks may sell their assets in the federal funds market.

T F 14. Commercial banks lend required reserves.

T F 15. The Federal Reserve lends only to commercial banks.

T F 16. If the Treasury issues new bonds that are purchased by the general public, the money supply is reduced if the Treasury deposits the funds in the Federal Reserve.

T F 17. If the Treasury sells gold to the general public and deposits the funds in commercial banks, the banks' reserves are not affected.

T F 18. If the Treasury runs a deficit and sells bonds to commercial banks, their excess reserves are reduced.

T F 19. Deficit spending is more inflationary when the Federal Reserve finances the deficit than when the general public finances the deficit.

T F 20. Inflation is measured by the Consumer Price Index (CPI).

T F 21. Recession is a period of falling prices.

T F 22. Unexpected inflation may transfer wealth from lenders to borrowers.

MULTIPLE CHOICE

1. The Federal Reserve
   a. is owned by member banks
   b. is owned by the Treasury
   c. lends to the general public
   d. borrows from commercial banks

2. The Board of Governors
   a. manages the nation's stock of gold
   b. has the substantive control over the money supply
   c. controls the U. S. Treasury
   d. is appointed by the U. S. Treasurer

3. The Federal Reserve's assets include
   a. corporate stock
   b. mortgage loans
   c. reserves
   d. government securities

4. The Federal Reserve's liabilities include
   a. gold certificates
   b. member bank reserves
   c. foreign currencies
   d. government securities

5. If commercial banks grant loans,
   a. the money supply is increased
   b. total reserves are increased
   c. excess reserves are increased
   d. the money supply is reduced

6. The multiple expansion will be reduced if
   1. commercial banks hold excess reserves
   2. there exists excess demand for funds
   3. borrowers withdraw cash
      a. 1 and 2
      b. 1 and 3
      c. 2 and 3
      d. all three

7. If funds are transferred from checking accounts to savings
   accounts, this will
   1. reduce commercial banks' ability to lend
   2. reduce commercial banks' total reserves
   3. reduce commercial banks' required reserves
      a. 1 and 2
      b. 1 and 3
      c. 2 and 3
      d. only 3

8. Commercial banks may borrow reserves from each other in the
   a. reserves market
   b. stock market
   c. bank market
   d. federal funds market

9. The multiple expansion of credit through savings accounts
   is larger than through checking accounts because
   a. savings accounts clear faster
   b. savings accounts are money
   c. the reserve requirement for saving accounts is smaller
   d. the reserve requirement for checking accounts is smaller

10. If deposits are withdrawn from a commercial bank,
    it may obtain the funds
    a. by liquidating an asset
    b. by liquidating a liability
    c. lending funds in the federal funds market
    d. lending funds to the Federal Reserve

11. The Federal Reserve may seek to expand the money supply by
    1. lowering the discount rate
    2. lowering the reserve requirement
    3. selling securities
       a. 1 and 2
       b. 1 and 3
       c. 2 and 3
       d. all three

12. The discount rate is the rate of interest
    a. banks charge customers
    b. the Federal Reserve charges banks
    c. paid depositors
    d. paid by the federal government

13. By selling securities to the general public, the Federal
    Reserve
    a. reduces the money supply
    b. raises commercial banks' deposits
    c. increases the money supply
    d. increases banks' excess reserves

14. The tools of monetary policy include
    a. open market operations
    b. the purchase of corporate stock
    c. the federal funds market
    d. taxation

15. If the federal government runs a deficit,
    a. taxes exceed expenditures
    b. expenditures exceed taxes
    c. receipts exceed taxes
    d. taxes exceed revenues

16. If the federal government runs a deficit and finances it
    by borrowing from the Federal Reserve,
    a. commercial banks' reserves are increased
    b. commercial banks' required reserves are decreased
    c. savings accounts are increased
    d. excess reserves are reduced

17. During a period of inflation, a federal government deficit should be financed by borrowing from
    a. the Federal Reserve
    b. commercial banks
    c. the general public
    d. the U. S. Treasury

18. If the federal government runs a surplus,
    a. taxes exceed expenditures
    b. expenditures exceed receipts
    c. revenues have declined
    d. revenues have increased

19. Anticipation of inflation encourages
    a. lending
    b. borrowing
    c. retiring debt
    d. saving

20. Recession is a period of
    a. falling prices
    b. higher employment
    c. rising prices
    d. increased unemployment

21. During a period of recession the Federal Reserve may
    1. increase reserve requirements
    2. buy government securities
    3. sell government securities
    4. lower the discount rate
        a. 1 and 2
        b. 1 and 3
        c. 2 and 4
        d. 3 and 4

22. Besides controlling the supply of money, the Federal Reserve
    a. manages the nation's gold stock
    b. clears checks for the nation's banks
    c. insures bank deposits
    d. grants commercial loans

23. During a period of inflation the Federal Reserve may
    1. increase reserve requirements
    2. buy government securities
    3. sell government securities
    4. lower the discount rate
        a. 1 and 2
        b. 1 and 3
        c. 2 and 4
        d. 3 and 4

ANSWERS TO FILL IN THE BLANKS

1. open market operations
2. purchases
3. sells
4. discount rate
5. member banks
6. Board of Governors
7. gold certificates
   federal government securities
8. decrease
9. majority
   Federal Open Market Committee
10. decreased
11. federal funds market
12. reduced
13. increased
14. deficit
15. not affected
16. general
    prices
17. Consumer Price Index (CPI)
18. recession
19. spending
    saving
20. nominal rate of interest
    rate of inflation
21. deflation

ANSWERS TO QUESTIONS/PROBLEMS

1. a. required reserves - increase by $20
      excess reserves - increase by $80

   b. required reserves - increase by $10
      excess reserves - increase by $90

   c. required reserves - decrease by $10
      excess reserves - increase by $10

   d. required reserves - decrease by $20
      excess reserves - decrease by $80

   e. required reserves - no change
      excess reserves - no change

   f. required reserves - increase by $20
      excess reserves - decrease by $20

2. a. demand deposits - decrease
      required reserves - decrease
      excess reserves - increase

   b. demand deposits - increase
      required reserves - increase
      excess reserves - increase

   c. demand deposits - no change
      required reserves - no change
      excess reserves - no change

   d. demand deposits - no change
      required reserves - decrease
      excess reserves - increase

   e. demand deposits - no change
      required reserves - no change
      excess reserves - no change

   f. demand deposits - decrease
      required reserves - decrease
      excess reserves - decrease

   g. demand deposits - increase
      required reserves - increase
      excess reserves - decrease

   h. demand deposits - decrease
      required reserves - decrease
      excess reserves - decrease

Chapter 5
INTERNATIONAL FINANCE

I. Foreign Currencies and the Rate of Exchange
   A. Demand and supply of foreign currency
   B. Foreign exchange markets
   C. Devaluation and revaluation
   D. Freely fluctuating exchange rates

II. Effect on Banks' Reserves and the Domestic Money Supply
   A. Checks clear through the Federal Reserve
   B. Currency inflows increase banks' reserves while
      outflows decrease reserves

III. Balance of Payments
   A. Current account
   B. Capital account
   C. Official reserve account
   D. Deficit in the U.S. balance of trade

IV. The Role of the International Monetary Fund (IMF)

V. Foreign Trade and Multinational Firms
   A. Benefits of foreign investments
   B. Foreign investments in the U.S.
   C. Financing foreign investments
      1. Eurobonds
      2. Selling securities abroad
   D. Risk and foreign investments
      1. Nationalization
      2. Loss from exchange rate fluctuations
   E. Risk reduction through hedging

SUMMARY

Demand for foreign goods is a demand for foreign currency. Foreign currencies (called foreign exchange) are traded in the foreign exchange market. Under a system of freely fluctuating exchange rates, the prices of foreign currencies change daily in accordance with the demand for and the supply of each currency.

If the value of a currency rises relative to other currencies, it is revalued ("appreciates"). The currency buys more units of other currencies making foreign goods and services cheaper. If the value of a currency declines ("devalued" or "depreciated"), the currency buys fewer units of other currencies making foreign goods more expensive.

Foreign transactions are cleared through the Federal Reserve. Currency outflows reduce the domestic money supply and the reserves of domestic banks. Currency inflows have the opposite effect; they increase the domestic money supply and the reserves of banks.

A summary of currency flows is given in the balance of payments, which enumerates what country's cash in and outflows such as imports and exports and international investments in financial and physical assets. Foreign travel, government purchases and grants, and investments abroad all result in currency outflows which are also recorded in the balance of trade.

When a country imports more than it exports, it has a merchandise trade deficit in the current account on the balance of payments. If a nation exports more than it imports, it runs a surplus in its current account.

When a nation runs a consistent balance of trade deficit or surplus, the value of its currency changes. Such devaluations and revaluations alter the demand for the nation's goods and services and help eradicate the surplus or deficit in the balance of trade. If the imbalance persists, the nation may borrow currency reserves from the International Monetary Fund.

Many firms have made foreign investments and have become multinational firms. Such investments offer the firm an opportunity to expand its markets or to produce its products more cheaply. There are, however, risks associated with foreign investments. Changes in the political climate, fluctuations in exchange rates, and special customs and laws may reduce or eliminate the potential profits a firm anticipates earning through foreign investments.

A firm may finance foreign investments through its traditional sources of finance such as retained earnings or may issue securities abroad. There is an active market in Eurobonds, which are bonds sold in foreign countries and may be denominated in dollars instead of the local currency. There are also active secondary markets in foreign countries for the stocks of many U.S. firms.

The firm may reduce the risk associated with fluctuations in exchange rates by hedging. If it has to make a future payment in a foreign currency, it may hedge by entering a contract to accept future delivery and buy the currency. Such a contract establishes the price of the currency, and thus the firm cannot lose if the value of the currency should rise. If the firm expects to receive in the future a payment in a foreign currency, it may hedge by entering a contract to make the delivery and sell the currency. The contract establishes the price at which the currency to be received in the future may be sold. The firm cannot lose if the value of the currency were to fall, since the sale price is established.

PROBLEMS

1. From the following information, construct the current and
   capital accounts for the U. S. balance of payments:
   Net income from foreign investments $5,000
   Foreign investments in the U. S.   6,000
   U.S. Government spending abroad   2,000
   Investments abroad by U.S. citizens   6,000
   Purchases of foreign securities   9,000
   Foreign purchase of U.S. Securities   7,000
   Imports   12,000
   Exports   13,000
   Was there a currency inflow or outflow?

2. If the price of the British pound is $1.40, how many pounds
   are necessary to purchase a dollar?

3. If the current price of a pound is $1.50 and the futures price
   is $1.53, how much does a firm pay to hedge against loss if it
   must make a future payment of 1,000,000 pounds and management
   hedges by entering into a futures contract to buy pounds (i.e.,
   to accept the future delivery of pounds)? If management does
   hedge, what happens if the price of the pound declines to $1.40?

FILL IN THE BLANKS

1. Foreign currencies are purchased in the _____.

2. Demanding foreign currency implies _____ the
   domestic currency.

3. If the demand for a foreign currency exceeds the supply,
   its price will _____.

4. The decline in the value of one currency relative to other
   currencies is called _____.

5. If a country's currency falls in price, that should stimulate
   _____.

6. If a country exports more goods than it imports, it has a
   _____ in its current account.

7. Special risks associated with investing abroad include
   _____ and _____.

8. Bonds issued abroad by American firms and denominated in
   dollars are called _____.

9. If a firm expects to receive a payment in pounds, it may hedge
   by _____ a contract for the future delivery of pounds.

TRUE/FALSE

T F   1. If a nation exports more than it imports, it has a
         surplus in its capital account.

T F   2. The demand for foreign goods implies supplying the
         domestic currency.

T F   3. From the viewpoint of international currency flows,
         foreign aid is essentially no different than
         importing goods.

T F   4. The current account of the balance of payments must
         always be balanced.

T F   5. While investments in foreign countries currently pro-
         duce currency outflows, they may generate currency
         inflows in the future.

T F   6. If a nation's currency rises in value, foreigners can
         purchase more of that nation's output.

T F   7. If the demand for a currency exceeds the supply, the
         price of the currency rises under a system of flexible
         exchange rates.

T F   8. Under a system of fixed exchange rates, the demand for a
         currency is fixed and cannot exceed the supply.

T F   9. The devaluation of one currency implies a revaluation of
         other currencies.

T F 10. If the American dollar is devalued, American goods are more
         expensive to people holding dollars.

T F 11. All nations may simultaneously have a balance of trade
         deficit.

T F 12. The International Monetary Fund may lend currency reserves
         to a nation with a deficit in its merchandise trade balance.

T F 13. Dollars deposited in foreign banks are called Eurodollars.

T F 14. The political climate abroad will affect the risk
         associated with foreign investments.

T F 15. Joint ventures between a firm and a foreign government
         may decrease risk.

T F 16. Bonds sold abroad by American companies denominated in
         dollars are called Ameribonds.

T F 17. Common stock issued by American companies is not traded abroad.

T F 18. If the firm expects to receive a future payment in francs, it can reduce the risk of loss by entering a contract for the future purchase (i.e., receipt) of francs.

T F 19. If a British firm expects to make a future payment in dollars, it can reduce the risk of loss by entering a contract for the future purchase (i.e., receipt) of dollars.

T F 20. If speculators expect the pound to decline relative to the dollar, they enter future contracts for the delivery (i.e., sale) of pounds.

MULTIPLE CHOICE

1. If a nation seeks to import goods, it
    1. demands foreign currency
    2. supplies foreign currency
    3. demands domestic currency
    4. supplies domestic currency
        a. 1 and 3
        b. 1 and 4
        c. 2 and 3
        d. 2 and 4

2. If a nation exports more goods than it imports, it
    1. has a favorable balance of trade
    2. has a unfavorable balance of trade
    3. experiences an outflow of currency
    4. experiences an inflow of currency
        a. 1 and 3
        b. 1 and 4
        c. 2 and 3
        d. 2 and 4

3. Which of the following causes a currency outflow?
    1. foreign travel and foreign investments
    2. foreign investments and military aid
    3. dividend payments from foreign firms
    4. domestic investments by foreigners
        a. 1 and 2
        b. 1 and 3
        c. 2 and 3
        d. 2 and 4

4. Which of the following causes a currency inflow?
   a. imports
   b. income from foreign investments
   c. military aid
   d. purchases of foreign securities

5. If a nation runs a surplus in its balance of trade, the value of its currency should
   1. rise
   2. fall
   3. not be affected
      a. answer 1
      b. answer 2
      c. answer 3
      d. answer can not be determined

6. Risk from foreign investments includes
   1. fluctuating exchange rates
   2. joint ventures
   3. possibility of nationalization
      a. 1 and 2
      b. 1 and 3
      c. 2 and 3
      d. 1, 2, and 3

7. If a firm has foreign investments in Germany and must make a payment in six months in marks, it can protect itself against a deterioration in the value of the dollar by
   1. entering a futures contract to sell marks
   2. entering a futures contract to buy marks
   3. entering a futures contract to buy dollars
   4. entering a futures contract to sell dollars
      a. 1 and 3
      b. 1 and 4
      c. 2 and 3
      d. 2 and 4

8. If a firm expects to receive a payment in liras after three months, the firm may hedge against a deterioration in the value of the lira by
   a. entering into a futures contract to sell liras
   b. entering into a futures contract to buy liras
   c. making payment now
   d. receiving payment now

9. Dollar denominated American bonds sold abroad are
   a. Eurodollars
   b. Eurobonds
   c. debentures
   d. foreign exchange securities

ANSWERS TO PROBLEMS

1.

	Credit	Debit
Current Account		
Exports	$13,000	
Imports		$12,000
Government spending abroad		2,000
Net income from foreign investments	5,000	
Balance on current account		$4,000
U. S. investments abroad		6,000
Foreign investments in U. S.	6,000	
Purchase of foreign securities		9,000
Foreign purchases of U.S. securities	7,000	
Balance on capital account		($2,000)

Balance on current and capital accounts is a currency inflow
of $2,000.

2. Pounds necessary to purchase $1.00:
$1.00/1.40 = .714$ pounds

3. At a price of $1.50, the cost of 1,000,000 pounds is $1,500,000.

At a price of $1.53, the cost of 1,000,000 pounds is $1,530,000.

The cost of hedging is $30,000 (i.e., the difference between
$1,530,000 and 1,500,000). For this $30,000 the firm is assured
that the price of the pound cannot exceed $1.53. If management
hedges and the price of the pound declines to $1.40, the gain on
the decline in the value of the pound is offset by the loss in
the futures contract, so there is no benefit from the decline in
the price of the pound. The gains and losses offset each other.

ANSWERS TO FILL IN THE BLANKS

1. foreign exchange market
2. supplying
3. rise
4. devaluation
5. exports
6. surplus (credit)
7. fluctuations in exchange rates, nationalization (political risks)
8. Eurobonds
9. selling

Chapter 6
THE ROLE OF SECURITY MARKETS

SUMMARY

Security markets take one of two forms: the organized exchanges (e.g., the New York Stock Exchange) or the informal market, the over-the-counter market. Listing securities on an organized exchange means that the firm has met certain specified requirements but not necessarily more worthy of investment consideration than unlisted stocks. The shares of many corporations trade through NASDAQ, the National Association of Security Dealers Automated Quotation system.

Specialists are market makers for stocks listed on an exchange. They provide an orderly market by standing ready to buy and sell securities at specified bid and ask prices. Markets in securities traded over-the-counter are made by security dealers. Specialists and dealers establish the spread between the bid and ask prices, but the interaction of buyers and sellers sets the general level of security prices.

Security markets are not financial intermediaries. The stock markets are primarily secondary markets in which securities are traded among investors. Firms receive the proceeds of security sales only when the securities are initially issued in the primary market.

Securities are purchased and sold through brokers. Securities may be delivered or left with the broker to be registered in "street name." Purchases may be for cash or a combination of cash and borrowed funds (on "margin"). Buying securities on margin magnifies the possible return but increases the risk of loss. The minimum margin requirement is established by the Federal Reserve.

Investors enter either long or short positions. In a long position the investor buys the stock in anticipation of its price increasing. In a short position the investor sells borrowed stock and antici-pates buying the stock back later at a lower price. In either case if the investor is right concerning the direction of the stock's price, the investor will earn a profit. Of course, if the price moves in the opposite direction, the investor sustains a loss. The loss (or gain) is a paper loss (gain) until the position is closed.

Fluctuations in stock prices are measured by various averages and indices of stock prices, including the Dow Jones industrial average, the S&P 500 stock index, and the New York Stock Exchange Index. Over time, stock prices have tended to increase.

Security markets are subject to regulation. The purpose of the regulation is to make certain that investors have access to information and can make informed decisions. These laws do not assure investors of earning a positive return on their investments. The federal security laws, called full disclosure laws, are enforced by the Securities and Exchange Commission (SEC). Investors are also protected from the failure of brokerage firms by the Securities Investor Protection Corporation (SIPC) which insures accounts with brokerage firms.

Americans may purchase foreign securities. They usually acquire ADRs (American Depository Receipts for foreign securities), which facilitates the purchase and sale of foreign stocks and bonds. American firms issue securities abroad that are traded on foreign security exchanges. Bonds denominated in dollars and sold abroad are called Eurobonds.

Security markets are very competitive. Security prices adjust very rapidly to new information. This competition and the speed with which prices change lead to the efficient market hypothesis which suggests that investors cannot expect to outperform the market consistently.

FILL IN THE BLANKS

1. A stock quote gives the _____ and _____ prices.

2. The difference between the bid and the ask is the _____.

3. The market maker for a stock listed on the New York Stock Exchange is called a _____.

4. An order to sell a stock at a specified price is an example of a _____.

5. After a security is purchased, the buyer must make payment by the _____.

6. After a stock is purchased, the buyer either takes _____ or leaves the securities _____ in street name.

7. An investor who expects a stock's price to fall and who does not own the stock sells _____

8. The margin requirement is set by the _____.

9. The New York Stock Exchange is an example of a _____ market.

10. The government agency that insures accounts at brokerage firms is the _____.

11. The federal security laws are enforced by the _____.

12. The purpose of the regulation of security markets is so that investors may make _____ decisions.

13. Purchasing securities on margin increases both the potential _____ and _____.

14. Americans who buy foreign stocks usually acquire _____.

15. The S&P 500 is a broad measure of _____

16. The theory that investors cannot expect to outperform the stock market consistently is referred to as the _____.

17. In an efficient market, price adjust _____ to new information.

TRUE/FALSE

T F 1. If a stock is quoted 20-21, an investor can buy the stock for $20 a share.

T F 2. The American Stock Exchange is an example of a secondary market.

T F 3. A purchase of 50 shares is an example of an even lot.

T F 4. The person who makes a market in a stock traded on the NYSE is called a dealer.

T F 5. After investors purchase securities, they must make payment by the settlement date.

T F 6. A major advantages of leaving stock registered with the broker is the custodial services provided by the broker.

T F 7. Capital gains taxes are paid only after the profits have been realized.

T F 8. The margin requirement for stocks is set by the Federal Reserve.

T F 9. An increase in the margin requirement may lead to lower security prices.

T F 10. The Dow Jones industrial average is a better indicator of stock prices than the Standard & Poor's index because it is broader based.

T F 11. The purpose of regulating the security markets is to increase investors' returns.

T F 12. The administration of the laws regulating security transactions is performed by the Federal Reserve.

T F 13. The use of margin increases the potential return on an investment in stock.

T F 14. Investors in foreign securities often purchase American Depository Receipts (ADRs).

T F 15. Security markets are often inefficient, so investors can anticipate beating the market over a period of years.

T F 16. Security prices tend to adjust rapidly to new information.

T F 17. If an individual establishes a short position and security prices rise, the investor sustains a loss.

MULTIPLE CHOICE

1. A specialist
   a. stresses one type of investment
   b. only buys stock
   c. analyzes corporate securities
   d. makes a market in securities

2. The New York Stock Exchange
   a. is a financial intermediary
   b. is a secondary market
   c. transfers funds to businesses
   d. forbids buying stock on margin

3. If the quote on a stock is reduced,
   1. supply exceeded demand
   2. demand exceeded supply
   3. some potential buyers leave the market
   4. some potential buyers enter the market
      a. 1 and 3
      b. 1 and 4
      c. 2 and 3
      d. 2 and 4

4. Entering an order to sell stock at $17 when the bid is 18-19
   a. is a market order
   b. illustrates a short sale
   c. requires a margin payment
   d. is a limit order

5. Buying stock on margin
   1. is an example of financial leverage
   2. is buying stock with borrowed funds
   3. requires leaving the stock with the broker
      a. 1 and 2
      b. 1 and 3
      c. 2 and 3
      d. all three

6. Over-the-counter stock quotes are obtained through
   a. NASDAQ
   b. SEC
   c. SIPC
   d. the specialist

7. Investors are insured against brokerage firm failures by
   a. SEC
   b. FDIC
   c. SPCA
   d. SIPC

8. If an individual sells a stock short,
   1. stock prices are expected to rise
   2. stock prices are expected to decline
   3. the investor sells borrowed securities
   4. the investor is realizing a short-term capital gain
      a. 1 and 3
      b. 1 and 4
      c. 2 and 3
      d. 2 and 4

9. The regulation of security markets
   a. discourages investing by requiring the registration of investors
   b. is enforced by the Federal Reserve
   c. protects investors from their own mistakes
   d. provides investors with information to make informed decisions

10. ADRs
   a. facilitate trading in foreign securities by American investors
   b. facilitate trading in American securities by foreign investors
   c. reduce the risk associated with fluctuations in exchange rates
   d. increase the risk associated with fluctuations in exchange rates

11. The efficient market hypothesis
   a. suggests that the market for securities is becoming less efficient
   b. implies that investor can consistently outperform the market
   c. is built upon competition and the rapid dissemination of information
   d. suggests that security prices change slowly over time

12. Which of the following is inconsistent with efficient security markets?
   a. stock prices change rapidly in response to new information
   b. investors cannot expect to outperform the market consistently
   c. bond prices change rapidly in response to new information
   d. analysis of financial data will lead to superior investment performance

13. Capital gains have no income tax implications unless
   a. stock prices rise
   b. stock prices fall
   c. the securities are given to another investor
   d. the securities are sold

ANSWERS TO FILL IN THE BLANKS

1. bid, ask
2. spread
3. specialist
4. limit order
5. settlement date
6. delivery, registered
7. short
8. Federal Reserve
9. secondary
10. Security Investors Protection Corporation (SIPC)
11. Securities Exchange Commission (SEC)
12. informed
13. return, risk
14. American Depository Receipts (ADRs)
15. stock prices
16. efficient market hypothesis
17. rapidly

Chapter 7
THE TIME VALUE OF MONEY

   I. The Future Value of a Dollar
      A. Funds earn interest - compounding
      B. Impact of time and the interest rate
      C. Interest table for the interest factor

  II. The Present Value of a Dollar
      A. Discounting the future back to the present
      B. Impact of time and the interest rate
      C. Interest table for the interest factor

 III. The Future Value of an Annuity
      A. Series of equal payments compounded into the future
      B. Annuity due and ordinary annuities
      C. Impact of time and the interest rate
      D. Interest table for the interest factor

  IV. The Present Value of an Annuity
      A. Series of equal payments discounted back to the present
      B. Impact of time and the interest rate
      C. Interest table for the interest factor

   V. Illustrations of Compounding and Discounting
      A. Decision tree to help determine which interest table to use
      B. Illustrations of problems involving the time value of money

  VI. Applications of the Time Value of Money

 VII. Nonannual Compounding
      A. Compounding more frequently than annually
      B. Adjustments of interest factors

VIII. Periods of Less Than One Year

  IX. Electronic Calculators

   X. Financial Calculators

SUMMARY

Funds invested today grow and compound as the interest previously
earned earns more interest. Funds to be received in the future are
worth less today, as these funds are discounted back to the present.

There are four cases: the future value of a dollar, the present value of a dollar, the future value of an annuity, and the present value of an annuity. An annuity is a series of equal, annual payments. If the payments are received at the end of the time period, the annuity is referred to as an "ordinary annuity." If the payments are received at the beginning of the time period, the annuity is referred to as an "annuity due." Determination of present and future value use interest tables that give the interest factors for future and present value.

The future value of a dollar and the future value of an annuity depend on the interest rate and the number of years. Higher interest rates and the compounding of the amount over a longer time period result in a higher future sum.

The present value of a dollar and the present value of an annuity also depend on the interest rate and the number of years. The higher the rate of interest, the lower is the present value of a future sum. The further into the future that the sum will be received, the lower will be its present value.

Compounding and discounting may occur annually (and the interest tables are constructed using that assumption) or may occur more frequently (such as quarterly or daily). The more frequent the compounding, the larger a given sum will grow as the previously earned interest is put to work earning more interest.

The principle of time value should be understood by investors as well as by financial managers. Many transactions involve the concept of the time value of money. For example, individuals own savings accounts or certificates of deposit, purchase securities, or participate in pension plans. Since all investments are made in the present but the returns are earned in the future, such investments involve the time value of money.

Time value concepts are applied to many decision in finance. Investments in plant and equipment, the valuation of securities such as stocks and bonds, the determination of the amount necessary to fund a pension plan, the construction of a mortgage repayment schedule are illustrations of real situations that require understanding of and ability to apply time value concepts.

While the text uses interest tables, financial calculators may also be used to determine the answers to time value problems. Since all time value problems have three knows and one unknown, the three knows are entered into the calculator which then solves for the unknown. Of course, the information must be entered correctly and the answers must still be interpreted by the user. The calculators, however, are exceedingly useful if the individual has many time value problems to solve.

SUMMARY OF EQUATIONS

Future (compound) value of a dollar:

(7.4) $P_o(1 + i)^n = P_n$

(7.5)   Interest factor: $FVIF = (1 + i)^n$

Present value of a dollar:

(7.6) $P_o = \dfrac{P_n}{(1 + i)^n}$

(7.7)   Interest factor: $PVIF = \dfrac{1}{(1 + i)^n}$

Future (compound) value of an annuity due:

(7.8) $FVAD = A(1 + i)^1 + A(1 + i)^2 + \ldots + A(1 + i)^n$

Future (compound) value of an ordinary annuity:

(7.9) $FVAD = A(1 + i)^0 + A(1 + i)^1 + \ldots + A(1 + i)^{n-1}$

(7.10) $FVAIF(i,n) = \dfrac{(1 + i)^n - 1}{i}$

Present value of an ordinary annuity:

(7.11) $PV = \dfrac{A}{(1 + i)} + \ldots + \dfrac{A}{(1 + i)^n} = \displaystyle\sum_{t=1}^{n} \dfrac{A}{(1 + i)^t}$

(7.12) $PVAIF = \displaystyle\sum_{t=1}^{n} \dfrac{A}{(1 + i)^t}$

(7.12n) $PVAIF = \dfrac{1 - \dfrac{1}{(1 + i)_n}}{i}$

Future value of a dollar (nonannual compounding):

(7.13) $P_o\left(1 + \dfrac{i}{c}\right)^{n \times c} = P_n$

Definitions of the symbols:

P_0 the amount (or principal) in the present

P_n the amount received in the future

n   the number of time periods (e.g., years)
i   the interest rate
A   the amount of the annuity payment
c   frequency of compounding

ILLUSTRATIONS:

(These illustrations use the interest tables which are rounded off
to three places. If you use other interest tables, a financial
calculator, or a computer program, your answer may slightly differ.)

The future value of a dollar: $100 grows to how much in six
years at 5 percent?

   $100(1 + .05)^5 = \$100(1.340) = \$134$

The present value of a dollar: $100 received after five years
is currently worth how much if the interest rate is 7 percent?

$$P_0 = \frac{P_5}{(1 + .07)^5} = \$100(.713) = \$71.30$$

The future value of an annuity due: $100 invested at the beginning
of each year for six years at 5 percent grows to how much?

   $FVAD = \$100(1 + .05)^1 + 100(1 + .05)^2 + \ldots + 100(1 + .05)^5$
   $= \$100(6.802)(1.05) = \$714.21$

(To convert the interest factor for the ordinary annuity into the
interest factor for the annuity due, multiply the interest factor by
1 plus the interest rate. For the discussion of this conversion,
consult the appendix to the chapter.)

The future value of an ordinary annuity: $100 invested at the
end of each year for six years at 5 percent grows to how much?

$FVOA = \$100(1 + i)^0 + 100(1 + i)^1 + \ldots + 100(1 + i)^{5-1}$
   $= \$100(6.802) = \$680.20$

Present value of an ordinary annuity: $100 received each year for five years is currently worth how much if the interest rate is 7 percent?

$$PVOA = \frac{\$100}{(1 + .07)} + \ldots + \frac{\$100}{(1 + .07)^5} = \sum_{t=1}^{5} \frac{\$100}{(1 + .07)^t}$$

$$= \$100(4.100) = \$410$$

Future value of a dollar (nonannual compounding): $100 grows into how much in five years if the return is 8 percent compounded quarterly?

$$FV = \$100(1 + \frac{.08}{4})^{5 \times 4} = \$100(1 + .02)^{20} = \$100(1.486) = \$148.60$$

(If the compounding had been annual, the final sum would have been $100(1.469) = $146.90. The difference between $148.60 and $146.90 is the result of compounding. This difference grows as (1) the frequency of compounding is increased, (2) the rate of interest is increased, and (3) the number of time periods is increased.)

PROBLEMS

1. AZ's dividend rose from $1 to $1.61 in five years. What has the dividend's annual rate of growth?

2. If a company paid a dividend of $1 in 19X4 and the dividend grows annually by 7 percent, what will be the dividend in 19X9?

3. If a college freshman wants a car costing $15,000 at graduation, how much must be saved annually if the funds earn 5 percent in a savings account?

4. If a college freshman can save $1,500 annually, how much will have been accumulated by graduation if the funds earn 7 percent?

5. If the gross private investment in the U.S. was $54 billion in 1950 and $136 billion in 1970, what was the annual rate of growth in the nation's investment during the period?

6. A company earned $2.00 per share in 1980 and paid cash dividends of $1.00. In 1990 it earned $5.20 and paid a dividend of $2.16. What is the annual growth rate in earnings and dividends? If the Consumer Price Index was 100 in 1980 and 163 in 1990, has the investor's purchasing power fallen?

7. If an annuity costs $200,000 and yields 7 percent annually for five years, how much cash can an individual withdraw each year such that the principal is consumed at the end of the time period?

8. A firm earns 10 percent annually on its investments. One possible investment offers $50,000 a year for ten years and costs $300,000. Should the firm make this investment?

9. You inherit a trust account that promises to pay $13,000 a year for ten years and then distribute $100,000. If current yields are 10 percent, what is the value of the trust?

10. If a creditor owes $24,000 and annually pays $3,000, how quickly will the loan be retired if the interest rate is 8 percent annually?

11. An annuity offers $1,000 for ten years. If you can earn 12 percent annually on your funds, what is the maximum amount you should pay for this annuity?

12. How much additional interest will you earn on $1,000 at 10 percent for ten years if interest is compounded semi-annually instead of annually?

TRUE/FALSE

T F   1. If interest rates are 9 percent, an annuity of $100 for ten years is to be preferred to $1,000 after ten years.

T F   2. If a bank pays 5 percent compounded semi-annually, the true rate of interest is less than 5 percent annually.

T F   3. If a person owes $50,000 at 10 percent and annually pays $10,000, the loan will be retired in five years.

T F   4. The present value of an annuity is worth more if interest rates are 5% instead of 10%.

T F   5. If an investor buys a stock for $5 and sells it after ten years for $10, the annual rate of return is 10 percent.

T F   6. A present value of a dollar table is constructed so that as interest rates rise, the numerical values of the interest factors increase.

T F   7. An annuity table is constructed so that as the number of years increases, the numerical value of the interest factors increases.

T F 8. In a future sum of a dollar table, the numerical values of
        the interest factors are positively related to the number of
        years and inversely related to the interest rate.

T F 9. In a present value of an annuity table, the numerical
        values of the interest factors are positively related to
        both the number of years and the interest rate.

T F 10. In a present value of a dollar table, the numerical values
        of the interest factors are inversely related to both the
        number of years and the interest rate.

T F 11. The interest factors in the present value of a dollar
        table are the reciprocal of the interest factors in the
        future value of a dollar table.

T F 12. Interest factors are a means to bring together the present
        and the future.

T F 13. In an ordinary annuity, the payments are made at the
        beginning of the year.

T F 14. The future value of an ordinary annuity will exceed the
        future value of an annuity due.

T F 15. Annuities due are worth more than ordinary annuities.

MULTIPLE CHOICE

1. The future value of a dollar
     1. decreases with compounding
     2. increases with compounding
     3. decreases with higher interest rates
     4. increases with higher interest rates
        a. 1 and 3
        b. 1 and 4
        c. 2 and 3
        d. 2 and 4

2. The present value of a dollar
     1. is larger the longer the time period
     2. is larger the shorter the time period
     3. is larger the greater the interest rate
     4. is larger the smaller the interest rate
        a. 1 and 3
        b. 1 and 4
        c. 2 and 3
        d. 2 and 4

3. An annuity due is a set of
   a. annual payments made at the end of the year
   b. equal, annual payments
   c. unequal payments made at the beginning of the year
   d. rising annual payments

4. Which of the following is the largest if the interest rate is
   12 percent annually?
   1. $100 compounded for three years
   2. $100 annuity compounded for three years
   3. the present value of $100 received after three years
      a. 1
      b. 2
      c. 3
      d. answer cannot be determined

5. If interest rates rise,
   a. the future value of a dollar declines
   b. the present value of a dollar rises
   c. the present value of an annuity falls
   d. the future value of an annuity falls

6. Interest tables may be used to help determine
   a. the amount of margin an investor pays to buy stock
   b. the amount of down payment to purchase a home
   c. the cost of an investment
   d. what an investment is worth

7. Interest tables may be used to help solve
   1. the growth rate in a firm's earnings
   2. the current value of an annuity
   3. the amount in a savings account after ten years
      a. 1 and 2
      b. 1 and 3
      c. 2 and 3
      d. 1, 2, and 3

8. Which is the smallest if interest rates are 10%?
   1. future value of $100 after four years
   2. future value of a $100 annuity for four years
   3. present value of a $100 annuity for four years
      a. 1
      b. 2
      c. 3
      d. answer cannot be determined

9. Interest tables cannot be used to determine
   1. commercial bank reserve requirements
   2. the growth rate in dividends
   3. the cost of an investment
      a. 1 and 2
      b. 1 and 3
      c. 2 and 3
      d. 1, 2, and 3

10. Discounting is
   1. the determination of present value
   2. the determination of future value
   3. expressing the present in the future
   4. expressing the future in the present
      a. 1 and 3
      b. 1 and 4
      c. 2 and 3
      d. 2 and 4

11. The time value of money suggests
   a. that the present is less attractive than the future
   b. individuals prefer a dollar in the present to a dollar
      in the future
   c. the present value of an annuity is negative
   d. annuities are worth less than lump sums

12. For investors, an annuity due
   a. is to be preferred to an ordinary annuity
   b. is worth less than an equal lump sum received at the
      end of the time period
   c. receives payments at the end of the time period
   d. produces unequal payments

ANSWERS TO PROBLEMS

1. This is an example of future value. Solve for the interest
   factor:

   $100(FVIF) = $161

   The interest factor is $161/$100 = 1.61
   Find 1.61 in the interest table for the future value of a dollar
   using five years. The growth rate is approximately 10 percent.

2. This is another example of future value:

   $100(1 + .07)^5 = X

The interest factor for the future value of a dollar at 7 percent for five years is 1.403. Hence

   $100(1.403) = $1.40

3. This is an example of the future value of an annuity. Restated the question is, what amount (X) times the interest factor for the future sum of an ordinary annuity of $1.00 for 4 years at 5 percent (i.e., interest factor = 4.310) equals $10,000?

   X(4.310) = $15,000
   X = $15,000/4.310 = $3,480

The freshman will have to save $3,480 annually to have accumulated the $15,000.

4. This problem is also an example of the future value of an annuity:

   $1,500(FVIF 7%, 4Y) = $1,500(4.440) = $6,660

5. This is an example of the future value of a $1.00.

   $54(1 + i)^{20} = $54(FVIF) = $136

   FVIF = $136/$54 = 2.52

The growth rate is slightly less than 5% annually.

6. These are all examples of the future value of $1.

   dividends: $1.00(1 + X)^{10} = $2.16; FVIF = 2.16
              X = 8%

   earnings: $2.00(1 + X)^{10} = $5.2; FVIF = 2.60
              X = 10%

   CPI: 100(1 + X)^{10} = 163; FVIF = 1.63
              X = 5%

The dividends and earnings have both grown more rapidly than the Consumer Price Index. The investor's purchasing power has improved (if it is assumed that the value of the stock has not declined to offset the gain in the dividends).

7. This is an example of the present value of an annuity of $1.00. The interest factor at 7 percent for five years is 4.10.

    (FVAIF)(X) = $200,000
    4.1X = $200,000
    X = $200,000/4.1 = $48,780

The person may withdraw $48,780 annually for five years.

8. This is an example of the present value of an annuity. The interest factor for the present value of the annuity of $1.00 at 10 percent for ten years is 6.145.

    X = $50,000 x 6.145
    X = $307,250

The firm should make this investment because the present value of the cash flow generated by the investment ($307,250) exceeds the cost of the investment ($300,000).

9. This is another illustration of present value, consisting of an annuity component and a single, lump sum payment.

    $13,000(6.145) + 100,000(.386) = $118,485

The trust is currently worth $118,485.

10. This is an example of the present value of an annuity in which the number of years is the unknown. Solve for the interest factor:

    $3,000(PVAIF) = $24,000
    PVIF = 24,000/3,000 = 8.

The number of years to retire the loan is slightly more than thirteen.

11. This problem is similar to #8 but is applied to an individual's investment. The present value of the annuity is

    PVOA = $1,000(5.650) = $5,650.

5.650 is the interest factor for the present value of an ordinary annuity at 12 percent for ten years. The investor should pay no more than $5,650 for this investment.

12. This problem illustrates the impact of more frequent compounding.

Annual compounding:

$$\$1,000(1 + .1)^{10} = \$1,000(2.594) = \$2,594$$

Semi-annual compounding:

$$\$1,000(1 + \frac{.1}{2})^{10\times2} = 1,000(1.05)^{20} =$$

$$1,000(2.653) = \$2,653$$

The difference in interest earned is $59.

Chapter 8
RISK AND ITS MEASUREMENT

I. The Expected Return on an Investment

II. Risk and Its Sources
   A. Diversifiable, unsystematic risk
   B. Nondiversifiable, systematic risk
      1. Market risk
      2. Interest rate risk
      3. Reinvestment rate risk
      4. Purchasing power risk (inflation)
      5. Exchange rate risk

III. The Standard Deviation as a Measure of Risk
   A. Dispersion around an investment's return
   B. Calculation of the standard deviation
   C. Expected return on a portfolio
   D. Risk reduction through diversification illustrated
   E. Importance of low correlation to achieve diversification

IV. Beta Coefficients
   A. Relative measure of risk
   B. Return on the stock relative to the return on the market
   C. Numerical values of beta
   D. Estimation of beta through regression analysis

V. The Capital Asset Pricing Model and an Investment's Required Return
   A. Risk-free return
   B. Risk premiums
   C. Use of beta coefficients to adjust for risk

SUMMARY

Investments are made in order to earn a return. The expected return depends on the anticipated return and the probability of its occurring. The expected return comes through income and/or price appreciation. The realized return, however, can differ considerably from the expected return which induced the individual to make the investment. This difference indicates the presence of risk. Virtually all financial decisions involve risk because decisions are made in the present but the results occur in the uncertain future.

One source of risk is the risk associated with the particular asset. For firms this depends on the nature of the business (business risk) and how the firm is financed (financial risk). This source of risk is often referred to as diversifiable or unsystematic risk. Diversification, which is the constructing of portfolios consisting of the securities of several firms in differing industries, reduces unsystematic risk.

In addition to unsystematic risk, the investor must bear non-diversifiable, systematic risk. These sources of risk include (1) the tendency for security price to move together (market risk), (2) the tendency for security prices to move in the opposite direction of changes in interest rates (interest rate risk), (3) reinvesting funds at a lower rate as a result of a decline in interest rates, (4) the loss of purchasing power from inflation (purchasing power risk), and (5) loss from fluctuations in the value of foreign money (exchange rate risk). While the impact of unsystematic risk is reduced by the construction of diversified portfolios, diversification has no impact on systematic risk.

Risk may be measured by the dispersion around an investment's return. This dispersion may be measured by the standard deviation. The larger the standard deviation, the greater is the risk associated with the particular investment.

An alternative index of risk relates the responsiveness of the return on the asset with the return on the market as a whole. This measure of risk is called a "beta coefficient." A beta of 1.0 means that the return on the particular asset equals the return on the market. A beta of greater than 1.0 indicates an aggressive asset whose return is more volatile than the market. A beta of less than 1.0 indicates a defensive asset whose return is less volatile than the market as a whole.

Beta coefficients measure past volatility and may not be indicative of future volatility. However, they may be helpful in constructing a portfolio consistent with an individual's willingness to bear risk. Beta coefficients are also used in the capital asset pricing model to adjust an investor's required return for the risk associated with the particular asset. Higher beta coefficients produce higher required returns, so that the investor is compensated for bearing more risk.

SUMMARY OF EQUATIONS

Return on a portfolio (r_p):

(8.1) $r_p = w_1(r_1) + w_2(r_2) + \ldots + w_n(r_n)$

Definitions of symbols:

$r_1 \ldots r_n$ the returns for 1 through n securities
$w_1 \ldots w_n$ the weights for 1 through n securities

Illustration: What is the return on a portfolio given the following information:

Stock	Return	Weight in Portfolio
A	10%	17%
B	-5	23
C	14	50
D	7	10

Answer: $r_p = (.17)(.1) + (.23)(-.05) + (.5)(.14) + (.1)(.07) = 8.25\%$

Required Return in the Capital Asset Pricing Model (k):

(8.3) $k = r_f + (r_m + r_f)beta$

Definition of symbols:

  r_f risk-free rate
  r_m return on the market

Illustration: If the risk-free rate of interest is 6.84 percent, and an investor anticipates that the market will rise by 12.5 percent, what is the required return on a stock with a beta of 1.34?

Answer: $k = r_f + (r_m + r_f)beta = .0684 + (.125 - .0684)1.34 = 14.42\%$

FILL IN THE BLANKS

1. Investments involve _____ because the future is _____.

2. Investments are made in anticipation of a _____, which may _____ and/or _____.

3. The return for a portfolio depends on the _____ of the individual assets and their _____ in the portfolio.

4. Individual stock prices tend to move _____.

5. The two measures (or indices) of risk are _____ and _____.

6. The standard deviation as an indicator of risk measures _____ around the return.

7. A beta coefficient is a measure of _____ risk.

8. Unsystematic risk is reduced through _____.

8-3

9. A beta coefficient of 0.8 means that a stock is _____ volatile than the _____.

10. The beta coefficient for a portfolio of assets tend to be more _____ than individual betas.

11. A stock with a beta coefficient of 2.0 is more _____ than the market as a whole.

12. Diversification has _____ impact on systematic risk.

13. Beta coefficients are estimated by using _____.

14. A beta of 1.4 will _____ an investor's required rate of return.

15. In the capital asset pricing model, the return on an investment depends upon _____, _____, and _____.

TRUE/FALSE

T F 1. In a world of uncertainty there would be no risk.

T F 2. Realized returns may differ from expected returns.

T F 3. The dispersion around an asset's return is one possible measure of risk.

T F 4. The larger an investment's standard deviation, the smaller is the element of risk.

T F 5. Systematic risk includes the tendency for a stock's return to move in tandem with the return on the market.

T F 6. Systematic risk is reduced through diversification.

T F 7. A beta coefficient indicates the systematic, market risk associated with an asset.

T F 8. A beta of 1.0 indicates that the stock's price is stable.

T F 9. The numerical value of a stock's beta coefficient is fixed.

T F 10. An aggressive investor will prefer stocks with high betas during declining markets.

T F 11. A portfolio consisting of securities that are highly correlated (i.e., very similar firms) is not diversified.

T F 12. Beta coefficients are computed with forecasted data.

T F 13. The expected return on a portfolio is a weighted average of the expected returns on the assets in the portfolio.

T F 14. Beta coefficients are reliable predictors of future stock price behavior.

T F 15. Conservative investors prefer stocks with low (less than 1.0) beta coefficients.

T F 16. Interest rate risk refers to the tendency of security prices to fall when interest rates rise.

T F 17. Stocks with low beta coefficients have higher required rates of return.

MULTIPLE CHOICE

1. Sources of risk include
   1. fluctuations in stock prices
   2. inflation
   3. possibility of bankruptcy
      a. 1 and 2
      b. 1 and 3
      c. 2 and 3
      d. all three

2. A diversified portfolio reduces
   a. unsystematic risk
   b. systematic risk
   c. purchasing power risk
   d. interest rate risk

3. The standard deviation measures
   a. the dispersion around an average value
   b. systematic risk
   c. unsystematic risk
   d. the security's high-low prices

4. A beta coefficient for a volatile stock
   a. is equal to 1.0
   b. is less than 1.0
   c. is greater than 1.0
   d. cannot be determined

5. A diversified portfolio may include
   a. only stocks of airline companies
   b. bonds of utilities
   c. stocks and bonds
   d. only shares of money market mutual funds

6. A beta coefficient is a measure of
   a. a firm's position in its industry
   b. the volatility of a stock's return
   c. aggregate market prices
   d. the volatility of earnings

7. A beta coefficient for a stock of 0.8 implies
   a. an 8% return on the market will cause the return on this
      stock to be 10%
   b. an 8% decrease in the market will cause the return on this
      stock to be 8%
   c. a return of 10% on the market will cause the return on this
      stock to be 8%
   d. a return of 10% on the market will cause the return on this
      stock to be -8%

8. An investor may reduce risk by
   1. selecting low beta stocks
   2. constructing a diversified portfolio
   3. selecting high beta stocks
      a. 1 and 2
      b. 1 and 3
      c. 2 and 3
      d. only 1

9. Which of the following is not a source of systematic risk?
   a. inflation
   b. reduction in the value of the British pound
   c. how a firm finances its assets
   d. a decline in the Dow Jones industrial average

10. The risk adjusted required rate of return excludes
    a. the stock's standard deviation
    b. the stock's beta
    c. the risk-free rate
    d. the anticipated return on the market

ANSWERS TO FILL IN THE BLANKS

 1. risk, uncertain
 2. return, income, capital appreciation
 3. expected return, weights
 4. together
 5. standard deviation, beta coefficients
 6. dispersion   7. systematic
 8. diversification   9. less, market
10. stable   11. more risky (more volatile)
12. no   13. regression analysis
14. increase
15. risk-free rate of interest, return on the market, beta

Chapter 9
INVESTING IN LONG-TERM DEBT (BONDS)

I. Characteristics of All Debt Instruments
   A. Interest and maturity
   B. The indenture and the role of the trustee
   C. Credit ratings
   D. Sources of risk
      1. Default
      2. Price fluctuations
      3. Loss of purchasing power

II. Types of Corporate Debt
   A. Mortgage bonds: bonds secured by real property
   B. Equipment trust certificates: bonds secured by equipment
   C. Debentures: unsecured bonds
   D. Income bonds: interest paid only if a specified level of earnings is achieved
   E. Convertible bonds: bonds that may be converted into the firm's common stock
   F. Variable interest rate bonds: coupons that change with changes in interest rates
   G. Zero coupon bonds: bonds sold at a discount whose value approaches face value as the bond approaches maturity
   H. High-yield bonds (junk bonds): bonds with low credit ratings
   I. Eurobonds: bonds issued abroad denominated in dollars

III. Registered and Coupon Bonds

IV. Determination of the Price of a Bond
   A. Bond valuation model
   B. Inverse relationship between a bond's price and interest rates

V. Yields
   A. Current yield
   B. Yield to maturity
   C. Comparison of current yield and the yield to maturity
   D. Using financial calculators to determine the price of a bond

VI. Retiring Debt
   A. Serial bonds
   B. Sinking funds
   C. Repurchasing debt
   D. Calling the debt

VII. Government Securities
   A. Federal government bills and bonds
   B. Tax-exempt municipal bonds

SUMMARY

Corporations may raise funds by issuing bonds, which are long-term debt instruments. These bonds require the borrower to make periodic payments (interest) and to repay the principal at some specified date in the future (the maturity date).

Corporations issue various types of bonds. Some are secured by liens on specific property (such as mortgage bonds and equipment trust certificates), and other bonds are unsecured (debentures) which are backed only by the credit-worthiness of the firm. Various types of unsecured bonds include variable interest rate bonds, convertible bonds, zero coupon bonds, and Eurobonds.

Bond prices fluctuate with changes in interest rates. When interest rates rise, bond prices fall. When interest rates fall, bond prices rise. The current price of a bond depends on how much interest it pays, how long before it matures, and what investors can earn on comparably risky bonds.

The current yield tells the investor the annual percentage earned on the bond. This yield does not consider any change in the bond's price that may occur if the bond is held to maturity. That is given by the yield to maturity, which considers not only the current price but whether the bond is selling for less than face value (i.e., at a discount) or for greater than face value (i.e., at a premium).

All debt instruments must be retired. Issues of bonds that all mature at the same time are called term bonds. Issues with bonds maturing at varying times are called serial bonds.

Some bond issues have a sinking fund which requires that the firm set aside a sum of money each year to retire the bonds. The issuing corporation may also retire bonds by calling them (if the bond has a call feature) or by repurchasing the bonds in the secondary market. Bonds may be called if interest rates have fallen and the firm can refinance the debt at favorable terms. Bonds may be repurchased if interest rates have risen and the bonds sell for a discount. In that case the firm can retire the debt for less than its face value and hence realize a gain on the repurchase.

In addition to corporations, governments issue bonds. The federal government issues a variety of debt instruments that range from short-term Treasury bills to long-term bonds. State and local governments also issue bonds. The interest paid by these bonds is currently exempt from federal income taxation.

SUMMARY OF EQUATIONS

The price of a bond:

$$(9.1) \quad P_B = \frac{I}{(1 + .i)} + \ldots + \frac{I}{(1 + .i)^n} + \frac{P}{(1 + .i)^n}$$

The current yield:

$$(9.2) \quad CY = \frac{\text{annual interest payment}}{\text{price of the bond}}$$

The current price of the bond (P_B) depends on the interest paid each year (I), the amount of the principal (P), and when the bond matures (n). The current yield (CY) depends on the annual interest and the price of the bond.

Illustration: What are the current yield and the price of a $1,000 bond that matures in ten years and pays a coupon rate of 6 percent ($60) annually if the current interest rate on comparable debt is 10 percent?

$$P_B = \frac{\$60}{(1 + .1)} + \ldots + \frac{60}{(1 + .1)^{10}} + \frac{\$1,000}{(1 + .1)^{10}}$$

$$= \$60(6.145) + \$1,000(.386)$$

$$= \$754.70$$

(6.145 is the interest factor for the present value of an annuity at 10 percent for ten years, and .386 is the interest factor for the present value of a dollar at 10 percent for ten years.)

The current yield is $60/$745.70 = 7.95%.

The yield to maturity is determined by using the same equation that is used to determine the bond's price (9.1). However, in the above application, the current interest is used (i.e., it is an independent variable) and the price is the dependent variable. When the current price is known and the interest rate is the unknown, the equation is used to determine this unknown yield which is called the yield to maturity.

The actual calculation of the yield to maturity is difficult because there is no simple means to solve the equation for the unknown. The unknown is part of both the interest factors for the present value of a dollar and the present value of an annuity. As is explained in the text, one means to solve is through trial-and-error. Also financial calculators and computer programs are available to solve for the yield to maturity.)

An approximation equation for the calculation of the yield to maturity is as follows:

$$(9.3) \quad i = \frac{I + \dfrac{P - P_B}{n}}{\dfrac{P + P_B}{2}}$$

If the price of a bond of $1,000 is $755, it pays annual interest of $60, and it matures after ten years, the approximate yield to maturity is

$$(9.3) \quad i = \frac{60 + \dfrac{1,000 - 755}{10}}{\dfrac{1,000 + 755}{2}} = 9.63\%.$$

(In the illustration above, the actual yield to maturity is 10 percent, so the approximate yield to maturity is off by 0.37 percent.)

PROBLEMS

1. A bond has the following features:
   Principal $1,000
   Coupon   9% ($90 per bond)
   Maturity   10 years

   What are the prices and current yields for this bond if interest rates on comparable debt are (a) 10% and (b) 7%?

2. If a $1,000 bond sells for $632, pays interest of $50 annually, and matures after twenty years, what is the approximate yield to maturity?

FILL IN THE BLANKS

1. Investors in bonds are subject to risk from _____, _____, and _____.

2. If interest rates rise, bond prices _____.

3. A company may force early retirement of a bond if it has a _____.

4. A debenture is an _____.

5. Convertible bonds combine _____ and _____.

6. A bond secured by real estate is a _____.

7. Periodic payments into a _____ will ease the retirement of a bond issue.

8. If the firm fails to meet the terms of the indenture, the bond goes into _____.

9. Bonds that are sold at a large discount and for which the firm does not distribute interest are called _____.

10. The current yield only considers _____, while the yield to maturity also considers _____.

11. Equipment trust certificates are illustrative of _____.

12. Bonds may be rated by _____ and _____.

13. A bond's value depends on _____, _____, and _____.

14. If a bond sells for a premium, its current yield is _____ the yield to maturity.

15. The interest paid by a municipal is _____ from federal income taxation.

TRUE/FALSE

T F 1. If interest rates rise, the prices of existing bonds increase.

T F 2. Bonds never sell for a premium over their principal value.

T F 3. The current yield on a bond is the interest (coupon) paid by the bond divided by the market price of the bond.

T F 4. The current yield is equal to the yield to maturity if the bond sells for par.

T F 5. If interest rates fall after a bond is issued, the yield to maturity will exceed the current yield.

T F 6. Since bonds pay a fixed amount of interest, their prices do not fluctuate.

T F 7. All debentures are bonds but not all bonds are debentures.

T F 8. If a convertible bond is converted, the firm's use of financial leverage increases.

T F 9. Bonds secured by collateral tend to be safer than other bonds issued by the firm.

T F 10. Bonds that are in default are given a B rating instead of an A rating.

T F 11. An equipment trust certificate is usually an example of a serial bond issue.

T F 12. A strong sinking fund implies the debt issue is riskier.

T F 13. A firm may retire bonds by purchasing the debt in the secondary markets.

T F 14. An equipment trust certificate is an example of a secured bond.

T F 15. If a bond sells for a discount, its price approaches the face value as the bond approaches maturity.

T F 16. The interest paid by federal government bonds is not subject to federal income taxation.

T F 17. The interest paid by municipal bonds is not subject to federal income taxation.

MULTIPLE CHOICE

1. The current yield on a bond is
   a. interest paid divided by the bond's price
   b. the bond's coupon
   c. the interest rate stated on the bond
   d. the yield over the lifetime of the bond

2. If a company fails to meet the terms of the indenture, it is
   a. bankrupt
   b. in default
   c. profitable
   d. in registration

3. Debt instruments subject their owners to risk from
   1. loss of purchasing power
   2. fluctuating interest rates
   3. default
      a. 1 and 2
      b. 1 and 3
      c. 2 and 3
      d. 1, 2, and 3

4. Which of the following bonds is supported by collateral?
   a. zero coupon bond
   b. mortgage bond
   c. debenture bond
   d. income bond

5. If a company enters bankruptcy court, bondholders should realize
   a. subordinated debt is paid off at face value
   b. convertible debt is superior because it may be converted into common stock
   c. all bondholders may lose their investments
   d. stockholders have the superior position

6. If interest rates in general rise,
   a. the prices of existing bonds rise
   b. the prices of existing bonds fall
   c. the prices of matured bonds rise
   d. the prices of matured bonds fall

7. If investors anticipate that interest rates will fall, they
   a. should buy bonds
   b. should sell bonds
   c. should buy shares in money market mutual funds
   d. should take no action

8. Bonds may be retired prior to maturity by
   1. repurchases
   2. a sinking fund
   3. a call feature
      a. 1 and 2
      b. 1 and 3
      c. 2 and 3
      d. all three

9. If a bond is selling for a premium, that implies
   1. interest rates have risen
   2. interest rates have fallen
   3. the yield to maturity exceeds the current yield
   4. the yield to maturity is less than the current yield
      a. 1 and 3
      b. 1 and 4
      c. 2 and 3
      d. 2 and 4

10. The current price of a bond is not affected by
    a. current interest rates
    b. the risk classification of the bond
    c. the maturity date
    d. last year's interest rates

11. Which of the following bonds are exempt from federal income taxation?
    a. zero coupon bonds
    b. debenture bonds
    c. convertible bonds
    d. municipal bonds

12. If interest rates decline after a bond is issued,
    1. the bond's price falls
    2. the bond's price rises
    3. the yield to maturity will exceed the current yield
    4. the current yield will exceed the yield to maturity
       a. 1 and 3
       b. 1 and 4
       c. 2 and 3
       d. 2 and 4

13. If interest rates rise after a bond is issued,
    1. the bond may be called
    2. the firm may repurchase the bond
    3. the current yield exceeds the yield to maturity
    4. the current yield is less than the yield to maturity
       a. 1 and 3
       b. 1 and 4
       c. 2 and 3
       d. 2 and 4

ANSWERS TO PROBLEMS

1. If interest rates are 10 percent, the bond's price is

$$P_B = \frac{\$90}{(1 + .1)} + \ldots + \frac{90}{(1 + .1)^{10}} + \frac{\$1,000}{(1 + .1)^{10}}$$

$$= \$90(6.145) + 1,000(.386) = \$939.05$$

(6.145 is the interest factor for the present value of an annuity of $1.00 at 10 percent for ten years, and .386 is the interest factor for the present value of $1.00 at ten percent for ten years.)

The current yield is $90/$939.05 = 9.6%.

If the interest rate is 7 percent, the price of the bond is

$$P_B = \frac{\$90}{(1 + .07)} + \ldots + \frac{90}{(1 + .07)^{10}} + \frac{\$1,000}{(1 + .07)^{10}}$$

$$= \$90(7.024) + 1,000(.508) = \$1,140.16$$

(7.024 is the interest factor for the present value of an annuity of $1.00 at 7 percent for ten years, and .508 is the interest factor for the present value of $1.00 at 7 percent for ten years.)

The current yield is $90/$1,140.16 = 7.9%

2. The approximate yield to maturity:

$$i = \frac{50 + \frac{1,000 - 632}{20}}{\frac{1,000 + 632}{2}} = 8.38\%.$$

ANSWERS TO FILL IN THE BLANKS

1. default, price fluctuations (change in interest rates), inflation
2. fall
3. call feature
4. unsecured bond
5. debt, equity features
6. mortgage bond
7. sinking fund
8. default
9. zero coupon bond
10. interest relative to price, price change
11. secured (or serial bond)
12. Moody's, Standard & Poor's
13. maturity date, interest paid, current interest rate
14. exceeds
15. exempt

Chapter 10
EQUITY: PREFERRED AND COMMON STOCK

I. Equity
   A. Represents an ownership claim
   B. Agency costs to link the welfare of owners and management

II. The Features of Preferred Stock
   A. Fixed dividend
   B. Cumulative dividends and arrearage
   C. Call features

III. Preferred Stock and Bonds Contrasted
   A. Preferred is riskier to holder
   B. Corporate dividend exclusion
   C. Tax deductibility of interest but not of dividends

IV. Analysis of Preferred Stock
   A. Times-dividend-earned
   B. Earnings per preferred share

V. Disadvantages of Preferred Stock

VI. Common Stock
   A. Voting for board of directors
   B. Cumulative voting
   C. Earnings are either distributed or retained
   D. Preemptive right to maintain proportionate ownership

VII. Dividend Policy
   A. Factors affecting dividend policy
   B. Income taxes encourage retention of earnings
   C. The firm's need for cash: earnings retention may lead to growth in the value of the firm

VIII. Cash Dividends
   A. The variety of payments
   B. The mechanics of dividend distributions

IX. Stock Dividends and Stock Splits
   A. Impact on the firm's balance sheet
   B. Impact on the value of the company and stockholders' wealth

X. Dividend Reinvestment Plans:
   A. Convenience and means to force saving

XI. Repurchase of Stock
   A. Alternative to paying cash dividends
   B. Reduction in outstanding shares

SUMMARY

Preferred stock and common stock represent ownership in a corporation. In small firms, management and owners are usually the same
individuals. In large corporations, the majority of stockholders are
not managers, and there exists a potential conflict of interest as
managers pursue personal goals at the expense of stockholders.

Preferred stock represents a prior claim to common stock. Preferred
stock differs from common stock in that its owners receive a fixed
dividend that is paid before dividends may be paid to common
stockholders. Preferred stock is often a perpetual security with no
maturity, and generally preferred stockholders lack voting power.

Since the amount of the dividend is fixed, preferred stock is
similar to bonds. Dividends are usually cumulative, which means that
if they are not paid, they accumulate, and these accumulated
dividends must be paid before any dividends may be distributed to
common stockholders. Preferred dividends, like common stock cash
dividends, are not a tax deductible expense. Thus, from the
corporation's perspective preferred stock is not an attractive
security to issue to raise funds as bonds whose interest is a tax-
deductible expense.

The owners of common stock have voting rights and a prorated claim
on the firm's earnings (after preferred dividends have been paid).
A corporation may retain and/or distribute its profits. Earnings
that are retained are invested and may subsequently increase the
value of the firm. Wealthy stockholders may prefer retention of
earnings to dividends since growth in the value of the shares
results in capital gains. The taxation of capital gains is deferred
until the gains are realized. Those investors who seek current
income may prefer that the corporation adopt a more liberal cash
dividend payout policy.

Stock dividends are not dividends but are a redistribution of the
equity accounts on the firm's balance sheet. While investors receive
more shares of stock, the value of each share is reduced to adjust
for the increased number of shares outstanding.

Stock splits have a similar impact on the firm as stock dividends.
Stock splits, like stock dividends, are recapitalizations which
alter the number of shares and the price per share. For example, in
the case of a two for one stock split, one old share becomes two new
shares, but the price of the stock is cut in half so the
stockholder's total wealth is unaffected by the stock split.

Corporate stock repurchases are another alternative use of the
firm's earnings. Such repurchases reduce the number of shares
outstanding. For the remaining stockholders, their prorated share in
the firm is increased.

Dividend reinvestment plans are a convenient means for the investor to accumulate shares. Such plans offer a savings on brokerage fees and are a means to force the investor to save.

FILL IN THE BLANKS

1. The possibility of a conflict of interest between management's personal goals and its fiduciary responsibility will lead to _____ costs.

2. Earnings are either _____ or _____.

3. Stock dividends have no effect on total _____, total _____ and total _____.

4. A two for one split will _____ the price of a stock.

5. Federal income taxes encourage _____ of earnings.

6. The ratio of dividends to earnings is the _____.

7. Retained earnings that are reinvested should produce _____ in the future.

8. If investors purchase stock after the _____ date, they do not receive the dividend.

9. One convenient means to accumulate shares is through a _____.

10. Preferred stocks usually pay a _____ dividend.

11. If a preferred stock is cumulative and the dividend is not paid, the stock is in _____.

12. Earnings per preferred share and _____ are two measures of the safety of a preferred stock's dividend.

13. Interest is a tax deductible expense but _____ are not tax deductible.

14. The repurchase of shares tends to _____ per share earnings.

15. _____ give stockholders the right to maintain their proportionate ownership in the corporation.

16. If a firm distributes a stock dividend, it reduces _____ but total equity is _____.

PROBLEMS

A company whose stock is selling for $45 has the following balance sheet:

Assets	$32,000	Liabilities	$10,000
		Common stock	6,000
		($6 par; 1,000 shares issued)	
		Additional paid-in capital	2,000
		Retained earnings	14,000

1. Construct a new balance sheet showing a 3 for 1 stock split. What is the new price for the stock?

2. What would be the balance sheet if the firm paid a 10 percent stock dividend (instead of the stock split)?

TRUE/FALSE

T F 1. Preferred stock dividends are usually fixed.

T F 2. Preferred stock dividends are tax deductible expenses.

T F 3. If a cumulative preferred stock's dividend is in arrears, the dividend is not being paid.

T F 4. Some preferred stocks have a sinking fund and must be retired at some specified time period.

T F 5. One measure of the safety of a preferred stock's dividend is the earnings-per-preferred share.

T F 6. A five percent stock dividend decreases a firm's assets.

T F 7. A cash dividend reduces a firm's equity.

T F 8. From the viewpoint of the stockholder there is no substantive difference between a 2 for 1 stock split and a 100 percent stock dividend.

T F 9. Corporations are obligated to pay cash dividends if they generate earnings.

T F 10. If a firm does not pay cash dividends, it may reinvest the earnings and grow.

T F 11. Cash dividends receive more favorable tax treatment than long-term capital gains.

T F 12. Stockholders who seek to defer taxes prefer capital gains to dividends.

T F 13. Most publicly held American firms that pay dividends tend to pay a regular quarterly cash dividend.

T F 14. When a stock goes ex-dividend, its price tends to decline by the amount of the cash dividend.

T F 15. A stock dividend increases a firm's retained earnings.

T F 16. Stock dividends increase the wealth of stockholders who receive additional shares.

T F 17. A reserve split (e.g., 1 for 10) should raise the per share price of a stock.

T F 18. Dividend reinvestment plans permit stockholders to defer income taxes on dividends.

T F 19. Dividend reinvestment plans are a convenient means to encourage individuals to save.

T F 20. Persons owning stock on the day a dividend is declared receive the dividend.

MULTIPLE CHOICE

1. Which of the following is not equity?
   a. paid-in capital
   b. retained earnings
   c. preferred stock
   d. convertible bonds

2. Common features of preferred stock include
   a. fixed, cumulative dividends
   b. variable, cumulative dividends
   c. fixed, non-cumulative dividends
   d. variable, non-cumulative dividends

3. Preferred stock and bonds are similar because
   a. they both have voting power
   b. the interest and dividend payments are legal obligations of the firm
   c. the interest and dividend payments are tax deductible
   d. the interest and dividend payments are fixed

4. Dividends may be paid in
   1. cash
   2. stock
   3. retained earnings
      a. 1 and 2
      b. 1 and 3
      c. 2 and 3
      d. 1, 2, and 3

5. A 10 percent stock dividend reduces the firm's
   a. stock price and retained earnings
   b. stock price and number of shares outstanding
   c. retained earnings and assets
   d. total assets and total equity

6. A stock dividend
   a. reduces the firm's cash
   b. increases the firm's total equity
   c. decreases the firm's retained earnings
   d. increases the firm's assets

7. Capital gains
   a. may result through the retention of earnings
   b. increase the firm's paid-in capital
   c. occur when the stock is split
   d. are inferior to stock dividends

8. If a firm pays a cash dividend,
   a. retained earnings are reduced
   b. additional paid-in capital is reduced
   c. the price of the stock rises on the ex dividend date
   d. income taxes are deferred

9. If a stock's price is $90 and the stock is split three for one, the price becomes
   a. $90
   b. $60
   c. $45
   d. $30

10. Dividend reinvestment plans are
    a. a convenient means to accumulate shares
    b. a means to defer federal income taxes on the dividends
    c. available only if the corporation distributes stock dividends
    d. more expensive than buying the stock through brokers

11. Stock repurchases
    a. increase per share earnings
    b. decrease per share earnings
    c. increase liabilities
    d. decrease liabilities

ANSWERS TO FILL IN THE BLANKS

1. agency costs
2. retained, distributed
3. assets, liabilities, equity
4. reduce (by 50%)
5. retention
6. payout ratio
7. higher earnings
8. ex-dividend
9. dividend reinvestment plans
10. fixed
11. arrears
12. times-dividend-earned
13. dividends
14. increase
15. preemptive rights
16. retained earnings, unaffected

ANSWERS TO PROBLEMS

1. Three for one split:

Assets	$32,000	Liabilities	$10,000
		Common stock	6,000
		($2 par; 3,000 shares issued)	
		Additional paid-in capital	2,000
		Retained earnings	14,000

The firm now has 3,000 shares outstanding with a $2 par value. The price of the stock adjusts to $45/3 = $15.

2. Ten percent stock dividend:

Assets	$32,000	Liabilities	$10,000
		Common stock	6,600
		($6 par; 1,100 shares issued)	
		Additional paid-in capital	5,900
		Retained earnings	9,500

The ten percent stock dividend results in the firm issuing 100 new shares. $4,500 ($45 x 100) is subtracted from retained earnings and added to the other equity accounts. $600 (100 x $6 par) is added to stock outstanding. The residual ($3,900) additional paid-in capital.

Chapter 11
VALUATION OF STOCK

I. Valuation of Preferred Stock
   A. Valuation model
   B. Impact of changes in interest rates

II. Valuation of Common Stock: The Present Value and Growth of Dividends
   A. Dividend-growth valuation model
   B. Return on the investment
   C. Different growth rates

III. Risk and Security Valuation
   A. Risk-adjusted required return
   B. Security market line relating risk and required return
   D. Changes in risk premiums illustrated

IV. Valuation of Common Stock: P/E Ratios

SUMMARY

The valuation of preferred stock is essentially the same as the valuation of bonds. The fixed dividend payment is brought back to the present (i.e., discounted back to the present). When interest rates rise, the value of preferred stock falls. When interest rates decline, the value of preferred stock rises.

The value of common stock depends upon the firm's dividend, the rate of growth in earnings and dividends, and investors' required rate of return. In its simplest form, the required rate of return depends on expected dividends and capital gains.

The required rate of return may be adjusted for risk. This risk adjustment considers what the investor may earn on a risk-free security plus a risk premium. This risk premium includes a premium for the market as a whole and for the systematic risk associated with the individual stock. This systematic risk is measured by the firm's beta coefficient. Higher betas lead to higher required rates of return which lower the value of the stock.

These variables (the dividend, the anticipated growth in the dividend, and the required return) are combined in the dividend-growth model which establishes a valuation for the stock. This value is then compared with the current market price to determine if the stock is overvalued (and hence should be sold, if owned, or sold short) or if the stock is undervalued (and hence should be acquired).

Common stocks may also be valued with the use of P/E ratios (i.e., the ratio of the price of the stock to per share earnings). These ratios are used as a multiple which is applied to estimates of the firm's earnings to determine what the firm is worth.

SUMMARY OF EQUATIONS

Valuation of preferred stock:

1. Perpetual preferred stock (P_p):

(11.2) $P_p = D_p/k_p$

2. Preferred stock with a finite life

(11.3) $P_p = \dfrac{D_p}{(1 + .i)} + ... + \dfrac{D_p}{(1 + .i)^n} + \dfrac{S}{(1 + .i)^n}$

Definitions of the symbols:

P_p price (or value) of preferred stock

D_p the fixed, annual dividend

k_p the required rate of return

n number of years until the preferred stock is redeemed

S par value of the stock which is redeemed in year n

Illustrations:

1. What is the value of a perpetual preferred stock that pays a fixed $1 dividend when the investor requires a return of 9%?

    Answer: P = $1/.09 = $9.09

2. What is the value of a $10 par preferred stock that pays a $1 dividend annually if the firm must retire the stock after ten years? The investor requires a 9% annual rate of return.

    Answer:

    $$P_p = \frac{\$1}{(1 + .09)} + ... + \frac{1}{(1 + .09)^{10}} + \frac{10}{(1 + .09)^{10}}$$

    $$= \$1(6.418) + 10(.422) = \$10.64$$

(6.418 is the interest factor for the present value of an
annuity at 9 percent for ten years, and .422 is the interest
factor for the present value of a dollar at 9 percent for
ten years. Notice that the value of this preferred stock
exceeds its par value: it sells for a premium, because the
comparable rate, 9%, is less than the fixed dividend rate of
10% of par.)

Valuation of common stock: Dividend-growth model for the
determination of the value of a common stock when the dividend
is assumed to grow at the same rate indefinitely into the future:

$$(11.6) \quad V = \frac{D_0(1 + g)}{k - g}$$

Definitions of the symbols:

  V   valuation of the stock
  D_0 the current dividend
  g   the annual rate of growth in dividends
  k   investors' required rate of return

Illustration: What is the value of a stock currently paying a
dividend of $1.50 that is growing annually at 8 percent when
investors require a rate of return of 12 percent?

Answer:

$$V = \frac{\$1.50(1 + .08)}{.12 - .08}$$

$$= \quad \$40.50$$

The rate of return on an investment:

$$(11.7) \quad r = \frac{D_0(1 + g)}{P} + g$$

The new symbols are

  r   the rate of return
  P   the price of the stock

Illustration: What is the return on the above stock if it is
purchased for $38 (i.e., for less than its valuation)?

Answer:

$$r = \frac{\$1.50(1 + .08)}{\$38} + .08$$

$$= 12.26\%$$

(Notice that the return of 12.26 percent exceeds the 12 percent required return because the stock is undervalued, that is, it is selling for a price that is less than the valuation.)

The risk-adjusted required rate of return from Chapter 8, i.e., the required return in the capital asset pricing model (k):

(8.3) $k = r_f + (r_m + r_f)beta$

Definition of symbols:

r_f risk-free rate of return
r_m return on the market

Illustration: If the risk-free rate of interest is 6.84 percent, and an investor anticipates that the market will rise by 12.5 percent, what is the required return on a stock with a beta of 1.34?

Answer: $k = r_f + (r_m + r_f)beta = .0684 + (.125 - .0684)1.34 = 14.42\%$

Illustration: using the risk-adjusted required return in the dividend-growth valuation model: What is the value of the above stock if the risk free rate is 8 percent, the return on the market is 12 percent, and this stock's beta is 1.4?

$$k = .08 + (.12 - .08)1.4 = .136$$

$$V = \frac{\$1.50(1 + .08)}{.136 - .08}$$

$$= \$28.93$$

Earnings multiple (P/E ratio):

(11.8) Value of the stock = Earnings x earnings multiple

Illustration: What is the value of a stock that is earnings $2.47 a share and the appropriate earnings multiple or P/E is 12?

Answer: $2.47 x 12 = $29.64

FILL IN THE BLANKS

1. The value of perpetual preferred stock depends on _____ and _____.

2. When interest rates rise, the value of preferred stock _____.

3. The value of perpetual preferred stock is more _____ than the price of preferred stock with a finite maturity.

4. The value of common stock depends on _____, _____, and _____.

5. The return earned on an investment in common stock depends on _____ and _____.

6. If a stock's beta coefficient rises, the required rate of return _____.

7. If the required rate of return declines, the value of a common stock _____.

8. The ratio of a stock's price to earnings is commonly referred to as the _____.

9. The dividend-growth model commonly assumes that a firm's dividend will grow at a _____.

10. If a firm's growth rate increases and the firm maintains its dividend, the valuation of a common stock _____.

PROBLEMS

1. What is the value of a preferred stock that pays an annual dividend of $3 a share and competitive yields are (a) 5%, (b) 10%, and (c) 15%?

2. What is the value of a common stock if
   a. the firm's earnings and dividends are growing annually at 10 percent, the current dividend is $1.32, and investors' require a 15 percent return on investments in common stock?
   b. What is the value of this stock if you add risk to the analysis and the firm's beta coefficient is .8, the risk-free rate is 9 percent, and the return on the market is 15 percent?
   c. If the price of the stock is $35, what is the rate of return offered by the stock? Should the investor acquire this stock?

3. What is the annual rate of return on an investment in a common stock that cost $40.50 if the current dividend is $1.50 and the growth in the value of the shares and the dividend is 8 percent?

TRUE/FALSE

T F 1. The value of a preferred stock rises when interest rates rise.

T F 2. Some preferred stocks must be redeemed at specified dates in the future, but that does not affect their valuations.

T F 3. The shorter the term of a preferred stock, the less volatile should be its price.

T F 4. An increase in the required return will tend to increase the value of a stock.

T F 5. The value of a common stock depends in part on the expected growth in dividends.

T F 6. The dividend-growth model determines what an investor thinks a stock is worth but not necessarily its price.

T F 7. The dividend-growth model assumes that the firm has an indefinite life.

T F 8. An increase in risk should cause the value of a common stock to fall.

T F 9. One index of systematic risk is a stock's beta coefficient.

T F 10. The risk-adjusted model for the valuation of common stock excludes yields on competitive securities.

T F 11. The dividend-growth model cannot be adjusted for changes in growth rates or changes in risk.

T F 12. A P/E ratio may be used as a multiple to forecast a firm's future earnings.

T F 13. Low P/E stocks indicate that the firm distributes a large proportion of its earnings as cash dividends.

T F 14. An increase in the yields on Treasury bills and other securities should depress the price of common stock.

MULTIPLE CHOICE

1. The value of preferred stock rises when
    a. interest rates and common stock prices rise
    b. interest rates and common stock prices decline
    c. interest rates rise
    d. interest rates decline

2. The value of preferred stock depends on
   1. the amount of the dividend
   2. the redemption date of the preferred stock
   3. yields on competitive securities
      a. 1 and 2
      b. 1 and 3
      c. 2 and 3
      d. 1, 2, and 3

3. If a perpetual preferred stock pays a dividend of $5 a year and yields rise from 10% to 12%,
   a. the price of the stock rises from $50 to $60
   b. the price of the stock falls from $50 to $41.67
   c. the price of the stock rises from $41.67 to $50
   d. the price of the stock falls from $60 to $50

4. According to the dividend-growth model, the value of a common stock depends on
   1. the price of the stock
   2. investors' required rate of return
   3. the future growth in dividends
      a. 1 and 2
      b. 1 and 3
      c. 2 and 3
      d. all three

5. An increase in investors' required rate of return will cause the value of a common stock to
   a. rise
   b. fall
   c. remain unchanged
   d. remain stable or rise slightly

6. When risk analysis is introduced into the dividend growth model, the required return considers
   1. the risk free rate
   2. the future dividends on the stock
   3. the firm's beta coefficient
      a. 1 and 2
      b. 1 and 3
      c. 2 and 3
      d. all three

7. A P/E ratio considers
   a. profits relative to earnings
   b. price of the stock relative to equity
   c. profits relative to equity
   d. price of the stock relative to earnings

ANSWERS TO FILL IN THE BLANKS

1. dividend, required rate of return
2. falls
3. volatile
4. dividend, growth in dividends, required rate of return
5. dividends, capital gains
6. rises
7. rises
8. P/E ratio
9. fixed rate
10. increases

ANSWERS TO PROBLEMS

1. Value of the perpetual preferred stock:

   a. at 5%: P = $3/.05 = $60

   b. at 10%: P = $3/.10 = $30

   c. at 15%: P = $3/.15 = $20

2. a $V = \dfrac{\$1.32(1 + .10)}{.15 - .10} = \$29.04$

   b. k = .09 + (.15 - .09).8 = .138 = 13.8%

      $V = \dfrac{\$1.32(1 + .10)}{.138 - .10} = \$38.21$

   c. r = $1.32(1+.1)/$35 + .10 = 14.15%

   The rate of return is less than the required rate (14.15% versus 15%) until the risk adjustment is made. After this adjustment, the expected rate of return exceeds the required rate of return (14.15% versus 13.8%); therefore, buy the stock.

3. r = $1.50(1+.08)/$40.50 +.08 = 12%

CONVERTIBLE BONDS AND CONVERTIBLE PREFERRED STOCK

I. Features of Convertible Bonds
   A. Convertible into stock
   B. Debt features: interest and maturity date
   C. Importance of the call feature
   D. Fluctuations in price

II. Valuation of Convertible Bonds
   A. The convertible bond valued as stock
   B. The convertible bond valued as debt
   C. The bond's value as a hybrid security

III. Premiums Paid for Convertible Debt
   A. Price in excess of the bond's value as stock
   B. Price in excess of the bond's value as debt
   C. Impact of the probability of a call

IV. Convertible Preferred Stock
   A. Similarity with convertible bonds
   B. Valuation as common equity
   C. Valuation as a perpetual preferred stock

V. The History of Two Convertible Bonds
   A. The American Quasar bond: rapidly called
   B. The Pan American bond: in existence for years

SUMMARY

Many firms have issued convertible securities (i.e., convertible bonds and convertible preferred stock) as a means to raise funds. These securities have the features of debentures and preferred stock, but, in addition, they may be converted at the holder's option into the stock of the issuing company.

Convertible bonds pay interest and must be retired at a specified date. They are also callable and may be converted into a specified number of shares of stock.

The value of the bond is related to both the stock into which the bond may be converted and the value of the bond as a debt instrument. As the value of the stock rises, so does the value of the convertible bond. The value of a convertible bond is inversely related to changes in interest rates. If interest rates rise, the value of convertible bonds falls.

Convertible bonds are, in effect, hybrid securities that offer investors the safety of debt (i.e., the interest is a legal obligation and the principal must be repaid) and the possibility of capital gains if the price of the stock into which the bond may be converted were to rise. Since the bond offers both the safety of debt and the possibility of capital gains, the bond tends to sell for a premium over its value as debt and a premium over its value as stock.

Once the value of the stock has risen, the company may call the bond for redemption. Since the redemption value is less than the stock into which the bond may be converted, such redemptions force the holder to convert the bond into stock. Thus the firm is able to retire the bonds without an outlay of cash.

Convertible preferred stock is similar to convertible bonds except that it lacks the safety of debt. While the convertible preferred stock does pay dividends and may be converted into stock, its features are not legal obligations of the firm, which implies that convertible preferred stock (like non-convertible preferred stock) is riskier to the holder than convertible bonds.

SUMMARY OF EQUATIONS

Value of a convertible bond as stock:

$$(12.1) \quad C_s = \frac{P}{P_e} \times P_s$$

Definitions of the symbols:

C_s value of the bond as stock

P_e exercise price of the bond

P_s price of the stock into which the bond may be converted

P principal or face amount of the bond

Illustration: A $1,000 convertible bond may be converted into 40 shares of stock (i.e., an exercise price of $25 per share). If the price of the stock is $44, what is the value of the bond in terms of stock?

Answer:
$C_s = \$1,000/\$40 \times \$44 = \$1,100$

Value of the bond as debt:

$$(12.2) \qquad C_D = \frac{I}{(1 + i)} + \ldots + \frac{I}{(1 + i)^n} + \frac{P}{(1 + i)^n}$$

Definitions of the symbols:

C_D value of the convertible bond as debt
I interest paid by the bond
n maturity date
P principal (or face amount) of the bond
i current interest on comparable non-convertible bonds

Illustration: What is the value of the above convertible bond if it pays interest of $70 (7% coupon) and matures after twelve years if the current rate of interest is 10 percent?

Answer (assuming annual compounding):

$$(12.2) \qquad C_D = \frac{\$70}{(1 + .1)} + \ldots + \frac{\$70}{(1 + .1)^n} + \frac{\$1,000}{(1 + .1)^n}$$

$$= \$70(6.814) + 1,000(.319) = 795.99$$

Convertible preferred stock's value as common stock:

$$(12.3) \qquad P_c = P_s \times N$$

Definitions of the symbols:

P_c value of the convertible preferred stock as common stock

P_s price of the common stock

N number of shares into which the preferred may be converted

Illustration: What is the value as common stock of a convertible preferred if it may be converted into 2.6 shares and the current price of a share of common stock is $57?

Answer:

$$P_c = \$57 \times 2.6 = \$148.20$$

Value of the convertible preferred stock as a non-convertible preferred stock:

(12.4) $P = D/k$

Definitions of the symbols:

P   value of the preferred stock as non-convertible preferred stock
D   dividend paid by the stock
k   investors' required rate of return on non-convertible preferred stock

Illustration: What is the value of a convertible preferred stock as common stock if it pays an annual dividend of $6.60 and investors require a return of 11 percent?

Answer:

$P = \$6.60/.11 = \$60$

(This valuation assumes the preferred stock is perpetual. If the stock is not perpetual and has a finite maturity date, Equation 11.3 in the text should be used to value the convertible preferred stock as a non-convertible preferred stock.)

PROBLEM

A firm has outstanding the following securities:

   Convertible debenture:
      Coupon   6.5%
      Maturity date   10 years
      Exercise price $20
      Principal $1,000
      Call price $1,065

      Convertible preferred stock
         Annual dividend $2.25
         Convertible into 2.5 shares of common stock
         Callable at $25 a share

Currently the common stock is selling for $13; the yield on non-convertible bonds is 10%, and the yield on comparable preferred stocks is 14%. (a) What is the value of the above securities in terms of the common stock? (b) What would be the value of each security if it lacked the conversion feature?

FILL IN THE BLANKS

1. The value of a $1,000 convertible bond in terms of stock depends on _____ and _____.

2. If the price of the stock rises, the value of a convertible bond _____.

3. All convertible securities have a _____ feature.

4. If interest rates rise, the value of a convertible bond _____.

5. The price of a convertible bond depends on its value as _____ and as _____.

6. A convertible bond may offer more safety than common stock because of _____.

7. The price of a convertible bond often sells for a _____ over its value as stock.

8. As the price of the stock rises, the probability of the bond being _____ increases.

9. The minimum price of a convertible bond is set by _____ or _____.

10. The conversion value of a convertible preferred stock depends on _____ and _____.

11. If the price of the common stock falls, the value of a convertible preferred stock _____.

12. A convertible preferred stock is not as safe as a convertible bond because _____.

TRUE/FALSE

T F 1. A convertible bond may be converted at the bondholder's option into common stock.

T F 2. Convertible bonds are often senior to the firm's other debt obligations.

T F 3. Generally, convertible bonds are callable.

T F 4. Convertible bond prices rise when interest rates increase.

T F 5. If the value of the common stock rises, the value of the convertible bond also rises.

T F 6. If a $1,000 bond is convertible at $100, it may be converted into 10 shares.

T F 7. The value of a convertible bond as stock depends in part on the bond's coupon.

T F 8. Convertible bonds tend to pay less interest than comparable non-convertible bonds.

T F 9. The value of a convertible bond as debt sets the maximum price of the bond.

T F 10. Convertible bonds tend to sell for more than their value as debt.

T F 11. As the price of stock rises, the probability a convertible bond will be called declines.

T F 12. As the probability of a call increases, the premium a convertible bond commands over its value as stock declines.

T F 13. As interest rates increase, the firm will seek to call its convertible bonds to avoid paying the higher interest rates.

T F 14. Convertible preferred stock is convertible into the company's debentures.

T F 15. Convertible preferred stock pays a fixed dividend.

T F 16. The value of convertible preferred stock varies with changes in the value of the firm's common stock.

T F 17. Convertible preferred stock is less risky to investors than the firm's common stock.

T F 18. Most convertible preferred stock is callable.

T F 19. If a convertible bond is not called nor converted, the firm must ultimately retire it.

T F 20. The cost to the firm of a convertible bond is less than a convertible preferred stock because the preferred dividends are not tax deductible.

T F 21. The most an investor in a convertible preferred stock can lose is the value of the common stock into which the preferred stock may be converted.

MULTIPLE CHOICE

1. Features of convertible bonds include
   1. fixed dividends
   2. call feature
   3. maturity date
      a. 1 and 2
      b. 1 and 3
      c. 2 and 3
      d. 1, 2, and 3

2. Convertible bonds have
   1. an indenture
   2. perpetual life
   3. a specified conversion price
      a. 1 and 2
      b. 1 and 3
      c. 2 and 3
      d. 1, 2, and 3

3. The value of a convertible bond as stock depends in part upon
   a. interest rates
   b. the maturity date
   c. the exercise price
   d. the call penalty

4. The value of a convertible bond as debt depends on
   a. the exercise price
   b. the call penalty
   c. the interest rate
   d. the price of the stock

5. Convertible bonds have a call feature to
   a. force conversion by stockholders
   b. force conversion by bondholders
   c. reduce the interest paid by the firm
   d. increase the interest paid by the firm

6. As the price of the common stock rises,
   1. the value of a convertible bond rises
   2. the value of a convertible bond falls
   3. the premium paid over the bond's value as stock rises
   4. the premium paid over the bond's value as stock falls
      a. 1 and 3
      b. 1 and 4
      c. 2 and 3
      d. 2 and 4

7. As the price of the stock rises,
   1. the premium over the bond's value as stock rises
   2. the premium over the bond's value as stock declines
   3. the premium over the bond's value as debt rises
   4. the premium over the bond's value as debt declines
      a. 1 and 3
      b. 1 and 4
      c. 2 and 3
      d. 2 and 4

8. Convertible preferred stock
   1. pays a fixed dividend
   2. may be converted into the firm's common stock
   3. is equity
      a. 1 and 2
      b. 1 and 3
      c. 2 and 3
      d. 1, 2, and 3

9. The value of convertible preferred stock as common stock depends on
   1. the exercise terms
   2. the dividend paid by the preferred
   3. the price of the common stock
      a. 1 and 2
      b. 1 and 3
      c. 2 and 3
      d. 1, 2, and 3

10. If interest rates rise and common stock prices fall,
    a. the value of convertible bonds falls while the value of convertible preferred stock rises
    b. the value of convertible bonds rises while the value of convertible preferred stock rises
    c. the value of convertible bonds falls while the value of convertible preferred stock falls
    d. the value of convertible bonds rises while the value of convertible preferred stock falls

ANSWER TO PROBLEM

Value of the convertible bond as stock:

First, determine the number of shares into which the bond may be converted: $1,000/$20 = 50 shares.

Next, multiply the number of shares by the price per share: 50 x $13 = $650.

Value of the convertible bond as debt:
$65(6.145) + $1,000(.386) = $785.43

6.145 and .386 are respectively the interest factors for the present value of an annuity and the present value of a dollar at 10 percent for ten years.

Since the bond's value as debt exceeds its value as stock, the bond will sell for at least $785.43, its value as debt. (The bond will probably sell for more than $785.43, as it will command a premium over the bond's value as debt.)

Value of the convertible preferred stock as common stock:
   2.5 shares x $13 = $32.50

Value of the convertible preferred stock as non-convertible preferred stock: $2.25/.14 = $16.07

Since the conversion value of the stock exceeds its value as non-convertible preferred stock, the convertible preferred stock will sell for at least $32.50, its value as common stock.

ANSWERS TO FILL IN THE BLANKS

   1. exercise price, price of the stock
   2. rises
   3. call
   4. falls
   5. stock, debt
   6. its debt features
   7. premium
   8. called
   9. value as stock, value as debt
  10. price of the stock, number of shares into which
      the preferred stock may be converted
  11. falls
  12. it lacks the legal obligation of debt

Chapter 13
FUTURES AND OPTIONS

I. What Is Investing in Commodity Futures?
   - A. The mechanics of purchasing futures
   - B. Commodity positions: long or short
   - C. The units of commodity contracts
   - D. Reporting of futures trading
   - E. Leverage

II. Hedging
   - A. Reducing risk from price fluctuations
   - B. Role of speculators

III. Financial Futures
   - A. Contracts for the purchase and sale of financial assets
   - B. The role of speculators and hedgers

IV. Stock Market Index Futures
   - A. Contracts based on stock indices
   - B. Use of by professional money managers

V. Options
   - A. Right to buy stock: warrants and calls
   - B. Right to sell stock: puts

VI. The Intrinsic Value of a Warrant or Call
   - A. "In" and "out" of the money options
   - B. Importance of the intrinsic value

VII. Leverage
   - A. Options magnify the potential return
   - B. Leverage increases risk
   - C. Time premium

VIII. Warrants
   - A. Issued by corporations
   - B. Factors affecting the time premium

IX. Call Options
   - A. Issued by individuals
   - B. Differentiated from warrants
   - C. Secondary markets: CBOE
   - D. Advantage of purchasing calls: leverage
   - E. Advantage of writing calls: income

X. Puts
   - A. Option to sell
   - B. Value increases as the price of the stock falls

XI. Stock Index Options

SUMMARY

Futures are contracts for the future delivery of a commodity such as wheat or U. S. Treasury bonds. These contracts are entered into ("bought" and "sold") by speculators who seek profits from correctly anticipating price changes and hedgers who use the contracts to reduce the risk of loss from price fluctuations.

Futures contracts are traded on commodity exchanges such as the Chicago Board of Trade. A speculator takes a long position (i.e., enters a contract to buy and accept delivery) in anticipation of a price increase. The same speculator may take a short position (i.e., enter a contract to sell and make delivery) in anticipation of a price decline.

A good faith deposit is required from the buyers and sellers of futures contracts. These deposits are called margin. The amount of margin is small relative to the value of the contract, so that small swings in the price of the commodity produce large percentage changes in the profits earned (or losses sustained) relative to the amount of margin. This ability to generate large returns is the primary appeal of commodity futures to speculators.

Financial managers use futures contracts to reduce the risk of loss. If a financial manager knows that the firm will have to buy a commodity in the future and may sustain a loss if the price of the commodity rises, the financial manager enters a contract to buy (to accept future delivery) and thus establishes a price. The contract to accept future delivery at the specified price reduces the risk of loss that would occur if the price were to rise.

If the financial manager expects to sell a commodity in the future, the firm could sustain a loss if the price of the commodity were to fall and thus it had to be subsequently sold at the lower price. The financial manager enters a futures contract to make delivery of (i.e., to sell) the commodity at the specified price, thus reducing the risk of loss that would occur if the price were to fall.

The futures price (as well as the current, i.e., spot price) are established by the demand for and supply of the commodity. It is the demand and supply of the various contracts by the speculators and hedgers that establish each contract's price.

While futures contracts initially applied only to physical goods, contracts have evolved for financial assets as well as physical assets. Today futures contracts exist for financial assets such as U. S. Treasury bonds and bills, foreign currencies, and stock index futures. All of these contracts are bought and sold by speculators who seek to profit by correctly anticipating changing prices and by hedgers who seek to reduce the risk of loss from changing prices.

Options give the owner the right to do something. A warrant is an option issued by a corporation that gives the holder the right to buy stock at a specified price within a specified time period. A call is an option sold by individuals (called "writers") that gives the holder the right to buy stock at a specified price within a specified time period. A put option is an option to sell stock at a specified price within a specified time period.

The value of an option is related to its exercise price ("strike" price), the value of the underlying stock, and the expiration date. If the price of the stock exceeds the strike price of a warrant or a call, the option is said to be "in the money." If the price of the stock is less than the strike price, the option is "out of the money".

Options are purchased by investors seeking to magnify the potential return. Since options offer potential leverage, they often sell for a time premium, that is, the price of the option exceeds its intrinsic value. Options are very risky and many individuals lose the entire amount invested in the option.

Individuals write options primarily for the income generated by the sales. These individuals may own the underlying stock, in which case they are covered option writers. Writers, however, may not own the underlying stock. If individuals write such "naked" options, they are taking large risks and may sustain large losses, if the price of the underlying stock were to move against them.

A put option is the right to sell stock at a specified price within a specified period of time. The value of a put option rises as the price of the underlying stock declines.

Options are actively traded on secondary markets such as the Chicago Board Options Exchange (CBOE). Besides options to buy and sell individual stocks, there also exist options based on the market which permit the individual to participate in movements in the market without having to select specific securities.

FILL IN THE BLANKS

1. If you expect a commodity's price to fall, you _____ a futures contract to establish a _____ position.

2. If you expect a commodity's price to rise, you _____ a futures contract to establish a _____ position.

3. Individuals who buy and sell commodity contracts in anticipation of price changes are called _____.

4. The number of contracts in existence is _____.

5. The good faith deposit required of buyers and sellers of futures contracts is called _____.

6. If a speculator's account has insufficient margin, the individual receives a _____.

7. By hedging the financial manager seeks to _____ the risk of loss from _____.

8. The current price of a commodity is called the _____ price.

9. If you have to purchase a commodity in the future and want to hedge against an increase in the price, you _____ a contract for future delivery.

10. A contract for the future delivery of U. S. Treasury bills is called a _____.

11. A stock index futures contract is sold (i.e., a contract to make delivery) if the speculator expects stock prices to _____.

12. If a portfolio manager owns a portfolio of stocks but wants to hedge against a stock market decline, the individual _____ a stock index futures contract.

13. A _____ is an option to buy stock issued by a corporation.

14. For an option to buy stock, the intrinsic value of the option is the difference between the _____ and the _____.

15. Because most options sell for a _____, the market price of a call option tends to exceed the option's _____.

16. At expiration the price of an option equals the option's _____.

17. If an individual does not own the underlying stock and sells a call option, that is illustrative of a _____.

18. An option to sell stock at a specified price is a _____.

19. The first secondary market in put and call options was the _____.

20. If the price of a stock is less than a call's strike price at the call's expiration, the option _____.

21. When a warrant is exercised, the firm _____.

PROBLEM

You are given the following information concerning a stock and a call option and a put option
    Price of the stock $32
    Strike price (both options) $30
    Price of the call $6
    Price of the put $3
    Expiration date   three months

1. What is the call's intrinsic value?

2. What is the time premium paid for the call?

3. What is the put's intrinsic value?

4. What is the time premium paid for the put?

5. If the price of the stock declines to $25, what is the maximum amount you could lose by buying the call?

6. If the price of the stock declines to $25, what is the maximum amount you profit by buying the put?

7. If after three months the price of the stock is $38, what is the profit (loss) from buying the call?

8. If after three months the price of the stock is $38, what is the profit (loss) from buying the put?

9. If the individual had sold the call naked and the price of the stock were $44 at the call's expiration date, how much did the writer lose?

TRUE/FALSE

T F 1. When a speculator enters a futures contract to accept delivery (to purchase), that individual anticipates taking delivery of the commodity.

T F 2. Investing in futures contracts is a safe investment because commodity prices are stable.

T F 3. The primary reason for selling a futures contract (i.e., making a contract to deliver) is the expectation of higher prices.

T F 4. A speculator who anticipates prices falling establishes a short position.

T F 5. Selling a commodity futures (entering a contract to make delivery) is a long position.

T F 6. A long position in a futures contract can be canceled by selling a futures contract (i.e., a contract to make delivery).

T F 7. The speculator must make a good faith deposit after entering a futures contract to sell.

T F 8. If a speculator has a short position and the commodity's price falls, that individual will receive a margin call.

T F 9. The amount of margin required to buy a futures contract is equal to 50 percent of the value of the contract.

T F 10. Hedgers enter commodity futures contracts because the contracts offer leverage.

T F 11. A financial manager hedges by simultaneously buying and selling contracts for future delivery.

T F 12. When a stock index futures contract expires, the buyer takes delivery of the securities.

T F 13. If an individual has a contract to accept future delivery of Treasury bills, the individual cannot close the contract without accepting delivery.

T F 14. If interest rates increase, the short sellers of U. S. Treasury bond futures profit.

T F 15. Speculators reduce risk of loss by buying instead of selling stock index futures.

T F 16. Warrants are issued by individuals.

T F 17. Call options are the right to sell stock at a specified price within a specified time period.

T F 18. The primary reason for purchasing an option is the income it generates.

T F 19. Put and call options actively trade in the secondary markets like the CBOE.

T F 20. If an option has no intrinsic value, it is "out of the money."

T F 21. Over time the "time premium" paid for an option tends to rise.

T F 22. The time premium tends to reduce the potential leverage a
        put option offers.

T F 23. At expiration an option will sell for its intrinsic value.

T F 24. An out of the money option will expire at the expiration
        date.

T F 25. The value of a stock index put option will rise if the
        market as a whole declines.

T F 26. A naked option writer owns the underlying stock that the
        call is an option to purchase.

T F 27. Naked option writing is more risky than covered call
        option writing.

T F 28. Stock index options are settled in cash.

T F 29. The writer of a put option anticipates that the price of
        the underlying stock will decline.

T F 30. Buying a put option is similar to selling a stock short;
        both positions anticipate a decline in stock prices.

MULTIPLE CHOICE

1. When a speculator invests in a financial futures, the individual
   a. enters a contract to make future delivery
   b. enters a contract to accept future delivery
   c. either enters a contract to make or to accept future delivery
   d. hedges to reduce the risk of loss

2. If the futures price falls,
   1. the short position sustains a profit
   2. the short position sustains a loss
   3. the long position sustains a loss
   4. the long position sustains a profit
      a. 1 and 3
      b. 1 and 4
      c. 2 and 3
      d. 2 and 4

3. The margin requirement for a futures contract is
   1. a small percent of the value of the contract
   2. a large percent of the value of the contract
   3. a source of leverage
      a. 1 and 2
      b. 1 and 3
      c. 2 and 3
      d. only 3

4. Hedging with commodity futures contracts
   a. increases price fluctuations
   b. reduces the risk of loss from price fluctuations
   c. increases the potential return
   d. does not require margin payments

5. Speculators take
   1. long positions
   2. short positions
   3. the opposite position of hedgers
      a. 1 and 2
      b. 1 and 3
      c. 2 and 3
      d. 1, 2, and 3

6. If a financial manager must sell output in the future
   that is currently being manufactured, that individual may
   reduce the risk of loss from a price decline by
   1. entering a futures contract to sell the good
   2. entering a futures contract to buy the good
   3. establishing a short position
   4. establishing a long position
      a. 1 and 3
      b. 1 and 4
      c. 2 and 3
      d. 2 and 4

7. If you anticipate receiving delivery of corn in the future at
   which time the corn must be paid for, you may hedge against a
   price increase by
   1. taking a long position in a futures contract
   2. taking a short position in a futures contract
   3. entering a contract to make future delivery
   4. entering a contract to accept future delivery
      a. 1 and 3
      b. 1 and 4
      c. 2 and 3
      d. 2 and 4

8. Which of the following statements are true concerning stock
   index futures?
   1. Stock index futures may be used to hedge against stock prices
      rising.
   2. Stock index futures require substantial margin and are a
      source of financial leverage.
   3. Stock index futures are settled in cash and not in delivery.
   4. Stock index futures are settle in specific securities.
      a. 1 and 3
      b. 1 and 4
      c. 2 and 3
      d. 2 and 4

9. A warrant
   1. is an option to buy stock
   2. is an option to sell stock
   3. is issued by individual investors
   4. is issued by corporations
      a. 1 and 3
      b. 1 and 4
      c. 2 and 3
      d. 2 and 4

10. The intrinsic value of a call option is
    a. the strike price plus the stock price
    b. the strike price minus the stock price
    c. the stock price minus the strike price
    d. the stock price minus the call's market price

11. At expiration, an option
    1. is worth its intrinsic value
    2. has no time premium
    3. may be exercised by the writer
       a. 1 and 2
       b. 1 and 3
       c. 2 and 3
       d. all three

12. A naked call option writer
    1. profits if stock prices rise
    2. profits if stock prices fall
    3. owns the underlying stock
    4. does not own the underlying stock
       a. 1 and 3
       b. 1 and 4
       c. 2 and 3
       d. 2 and 4

13. When a call option is exercised,
    a. the firm issues new stock
    b. the writer supplies the stock
    c. the firm's earnings are diluted
    d. the option is converted into stock

14. An investor who writes a call option closes the position by
    a. purchasing the stock
    b. selling the option
    c. letting the option expire
    d. repurchasing the option

15. The buyer of a put option
    a. expects prices to rise
    b. expects prices to fall
    c. owns the underlying stock
    d. does not own the underlying stock

ANSWERS TO FILL IN THE BLANKS

 1. sell, short
 2. buy, long
 3. speculators
 4. the open interest
 5. margin
 6. margin call
 7. reduce, price fluctuations
 8. spot
 9. buy (enter a contract to accept delivery)
10. financial futures
11. fall
12. sells (enters a contract to make delivery)
13. warrant
14. price of the stock, strike price (exercise price)
15. time premium, intrinsic value
16. intrinsic value
17. naked option
18. put
19. Chicago Board Options Exchange (CBOE)
20. expires
21. issues new shares

ANSWERS TO PROBLEM

1. Intrinsic value: $32 - 30 = $2
2. Time premium: $6 - 2 = $4
3. Intrinsic value: $30 -32 = nil; ($0)
4. Time premium: $3 - 0 = $3
5. Maximum loss from buying the call: $6
6. Intrinsic value: $38 - 30 = $8
   Profit: $8 - 6 = $2
7. Maximum profit from buying the put: 2
8. Intrinsic value: $30 - 38 = nil; ($0)
   Loss: $0 - 3 = ($3)
9. Intrinsic value: $44 - 30 = $14
   Loss: $6 - (14) = ($8)

I. Investment Companies: Origins and Terminology
   A. Closed-end investment company
   B. Open-end investment company (mutual fund)
   C. Rationale for investment companies
   D. Taxation of investment companies
   E. Net asset value

II. Closed-end Investment Companies
   A. Shares traded in the secondary markets
   B. Sources of return
   C. Costs associated with

III. Unit Trusts

IV. Mutual funds
   A. Shares are purchased from and redeemed to the mutual fund
   B. Loading fees (sales charges)
   C. Sources of return and risk
   D. The portfolios of mutual funds
      1. Growth funds
      2. Special situation funds
      3. Balanced funds
   E. The portfolios of specialized funds
   F. Index funds

V. Mutual Funds with Foreign Investments

VI. The Returns Earned on Investments in Mutual Funds

SUMMARY

Instead of directly acquiring stocks and bonds, some investors prefer to acquire shares in investment companies. These companies take the proceeds of the sales of their shares and use the funds to acquire financial assets. Closed-end investment companies have a specified number of shares outstanding which are bought and sold on the secondary markets as the stock or bonds of AT&T are bought and sold. Open-end investment companies (mutual funds) do not have a set capital structure. They issue new shares when individuals seek to invest in the funds and redeem (i.e., repurchase) the shares when individuals seek to sell them.

The book value of an investment company's stock is its net asset value. The shares of closed-end investment companies may sell for a premium over or a discount from the net asset value.

The shares of mutual funds can never sell for a discount from net asset value and often sell their shares for a premium, called a "loading" fee which is in effect a commission charged for purchasing the shares.

Returns from investment companies come from income earned and/or from capital gains. The funds are a conduit through which income and capital gains are passed to stockholders. The investment companies pay no federal income tax. Instead the stockholders are responsible for paying the appropriate federal income taxes on the earnings and capital gains generated by the investment company.

The costs associated with investing in mutual funds include loading fees, commission when the funds buy and sell securities, and management fees. The advantages offered by investment companies include professional management and custodial services. For many investors the primary advantage offerred by mutual funds is instant diversification, since many funds own diversified portfolios of securities.

While investment companies have diversified portfolios, they also have a specified goal such as income or growth (i.e., capital appreciation). Some funds seek investments in special situations or government securities, and some funds have very specialized portfolios such as the money market mutual funds, the index funds, or the sector funds.

The managements of investment companies make investments in the efficient financial markets. Few managements are able to outperform the market consistently. The funds, however, do relieve the investor of having to decide on specific stocks and bonds and they do offer the important advantage of diversification.

FILL IN THE BLANKS

1. An investment company with a specified number of shares is called _____.

2. Mutual funds issue new shares when individuals invest and agree to _____ the shares on demand.

3. A mutual fund's sales fee is called a _____.

4. The shares of a closed-end investment company may sell for a _____ or a _____ from the firm's _____.

5. A closed-end investment company with a fixed portfolio is called a _____.

6. A mutual fund redeems its shares at the shares' _____.

7. Perhaps the most important advantage offered by mutual funds to an investor with a modest amount to invest is _____.

8. A mutual funds whose portfolio seeks to duplicate a measure of the market is called an _____.

9. Investment companies with foreign investments include _____ which hold only foreign securities and _____ which hold both foreign and U.S. securities.

10. That few investment company managers are able to outperform the market consistently is compatible with the _____.

TRUE/FALSE

T F 1. The shares of mutual funds are readily bought and sold in efficient, secondary markets.

T F 2. The shares of closed-end investment companies are bought and sold in secondary markets like the NYSE.

T F 3. The shares of closed-end investment companies generally sell for a premium and rarely sell for a discount.

T F 4. The shares of mutual funds cannot sell for a discount.

T F 5. Mutual funds repurchase shares at their net asset value.

T F 6. Mutual funds distribute capital gains they realize but retain the income they earn.

T F 7. Mutual funds pay federal income taxes on dividends they receive from their investments.

T F 8. Loading fees reduce the investor's return.

T F 9. Mutual funds are subject to regulation by the Securities and Exchange Commission (SEC).

T F 10. Closed-end investment companies do not charge loading fees.

T F 11. The loading fee reduces a fund's net asset value.

T F 12. Purchases of shares in mutual funds reduce systematic and unsystematic risk.

T F 13. U.S. mutual funds may not hold foreign securities.

T F 14. An index fund seeks to outperform a specific stock index like the S&P 500.

MULTIPLE CHOICE

1. Types of investment companies include
    1. closed-end investment companies
    2. unit trusts
    3. mutual funds
        a. 1 and 2
        b. 1 and 3
        c. 2 and 3
        d. all three

2. The net assets value of a mutual fund's share increases with
    a. an increase in loading fees
    b. an increase in interest rates
    c. an increase in security prices
    d. an increase in the fund's assets

3. Sources of return to investors in a growth fund include
    1. possible capital gains
    2. tax savings
    3. possible income
    4. no management fees
        a. 1 and 2
        b. 1 and 3
        c. 2 and 3
        d. 2 and 4

4. Advantages associated with investing in mutual funds do not include
    a. diversification
    b. professional management
    c. custodial services
    d. reduction in interest rate risk

5. The shares of mutual funds are bought
    a. in the secondary markets
    b. from closed-end investment companies
    c. from commercial banks
    d. from the mutual fund

6. An index fund limits its portfolio to
    a. high quality stock and bonds
    b. stocks that respond to changes in the Consumer Price Index
    c. stocks of firms in a particular industry
    d. stocks included in an aggregate measure of the stock market

7. Which of the following is not an investment company?
    a. money market mutual fund
    b. a unit trust
    c. a brokerage firm
    d. First Australian Income Fund

8. No load funds
   a. have no selling fees
   b. pay no cash dividends
   c. have no administrative expenses
   d. have a fixed portfolio

9. Which of the following is not an example of a specialized fund?
   a. an index fund
   b. a money market mutual fund
   c. a balanced fund
   d. The Mexico Fund

10. Diversified growth funds reduce which source of risk?
    a. interest rate risk
    b. business risk
    c. exchange rate risk
    d. systematic risk

11. The efficient market hypothesis suggests that
    1. professional portfolio managers will outperform the individual investor
    2. professional portfolio managers will not outperform the individual investor
    3. professional portfolio managers will consistently outperform the market
    4. professional portfolio managers will not consistently outperform the market
       a. 1 and 3
       b. 1 and 4
       c. 2 and 3
       d. 2 and 4

ANSWERS TO FILL IN THE BLANKS

1. a closed-end investment company
2. redeem (repurchase)
3. loading charge
4. premium, discount, net asset value
5. unit trust
6. net asset value
7. diversification
8. index fund
9. international funds, global funds
10. efficient market hypothesis

Chapter 15
THE FORMS OF BUSINESS AND FEDERAL INCOME TAXATION

   I. Forms of Businesses
      A. Sole proprietorships
      B. Partnerships
      C. Corporations
         1. Legal entity and limited liability
         2. Transferability
         3. Permanence

  II. Taxes
      A. Progressivity of taxes
      B. Marginal tax rates
      C. Differences in tax rates and the decision to incorporate
      D. Reinvestment of earnings argues for the corporate
         form of business

 III. S Corporations

  IV. Other Tax Considerations: Fringe Benefits

   V. Depreciation
      A. Straight-line
      B. Accelerated depreciation
      C. Impact on earnings and taxes
      D. Added back to income to determine cash flow
      F. Modified accelerated cost recovery system (MACRS)
      G. Methods of depreciation compared

  VI. Losses and Tax Savings
      A. Corporate tax losses offset income
      B. Carry losses back three years and forward up to fifteen
         years

SUMMARY

There are three major forms of businesses. Sole proprietorships
(i.e., one owner) are the largest in number. The other major forms
are partnerships and corporations. In terms of revenues, assets, and
earnings corporations are by far the largest form of business.

Corporations are legal entities that are created by a state. The
advantages associated with the corporate form of business include
limited liability (at least for publicly held corporations), ease of
transfer of title, and permanence. Corporations are taxed
differently than sole proprietorships and partnerships, which are
not taxed. Instead, the owners are subject to the tax on the firm's
earnings. Corporations, however, have their earnings taxed, and
these earnings are taxed again if they are distributed as dividends.
(S corporations, however, are taxed as if they were partnerships.)

Taxes and their impact on the firm are a major concern of the financial manager. Taxes may be progressive, proportionate, or regressive. If the tax rate increases as the tax base increases, the tax is progressive. If the tax rate declines as the tax base increases, the tax is regressive. If the tax rate is constant, then the tax is proportionate.

The decision to incorporate is often influenced by taxation and the need to raise funds to grow. If the owners of a firm seek to expand and reinvest earnings in the business, the corporate form is usually the preferred form of business enterprise.

Depreciation is the gradual wearing away (i.e., consuming) of an asset over time. Long-term assets are used over several years and this consumption of the asset is accounted for through depreciation expense. Depreciation is the allocation of the cost over a period of time such as the life of the asset. Depreciation is a non-cash expense in that it does not require an outlay of cash. Since depreciation is a non-cash expense, it is added back to the firm's earnings to determine cash flow from operations.

Depreciation expense usually takes one of two forms: straight-line or accelerated. Straight-line depreciation decreases the asset's value by the same amount each year. Accelerated depreciation reduces the value of an asset by a larger proportion during its earlier life and a smaller proportion during its later years. The accepted method of accelerated depreciation is the modified accelerated cost recovery system (MACRS) in which a percent of an asset's cost is depreciated each year depending on the class of the asset (for example, 5 years, 7 years, or 10 years).

While management seeks to operate at a profit, firms may generate a loss. For corporations losses in one year are used to offset income in other years. Initially, the loss is carried back three years to offset income previously earned. If this income is less than the loss, the remaining loss is carried forward for up to fifteen years.

FILL IN THE BLANKS

1. The most common forms of business are _____,
   _____, and _____.

2. Ease of transferring _____ is one advantage of
   _____; _____ liability is another.

3. Corporations receive charters from a _____.
   The relationship between a corporation and its stockholders
   is specified in the _____.

4. If the tax rate declines as the tax base declines, the tax is _____.

5. A corporation that is taxed as if it were a partnership is referred to as an _____.

6. The general partners in a limited partnership generally have _____ liability.

7. The tax rate on the last dollar of income is the _____ tax rate.

8. Realized profits on investments in common stock are taxed as _____ gains.

9. The allocation of the cost of an investment over a period of time is _____.

10. The two general forms of depreciation are _____ and _____.

11. Accelerated depreciation initially reduces the firm's _____ and _____.

12. To determine the firm's cash flow from operations, depreciation expense is _____ to net income.

13. Depreciation expense does not start until an asset has been in place for more than _____.

14. Corporate tax losses are carried back _____ and then carried forward for up to _____.

15. If a corporation has been profitable and then operates at a loss, it should receive a _____ from the IRS.

TRUE/FALSE

T F 1. Partnerships constitute the largest number of business and generate the most profits.

T F 2. If one's income tax rate declines as income declines, the tax is regressive.

T F 3. If your income rises and your tax rate rises, you may conclude that the tax is progressive.

T F 4. Limited liability may not apply for small corporations if the owners pledge their personal assets to secure a loan for the firm.

T F   5. An investor can transfer ownership in a corporation to another individual.

T F   6. The voting rights of stockholders are specified in the corporation's bylaws.

T F   7. It is not possible to have limited liability in a partnership.

T F   8. Since a corporation is created by a state, its owners must live in that state.

T F   9. Since a corporation is responsible for its debts, creditors may not sue the stockholders of publicly-held corporations.

T F 10. If a partner dies, the partnership may cease to exist, but if a stockholder dies, the corporation continues to exist.

T F 11. An S corporation is taxed in the same manner as other corporations are taxed.

T F 12. Federal personal income tax rates are regressive.

T F 13. Federal taxes on long-term capital gains are more than federal taxes on an equal amount of ordinary income.

T F 14. The federal income tax laws encourage the retention of earnings by corporations.

T F 15. If a firm uses accelerated depreciation, its profits are initially decreased.

T F 16. If the cost of equipment is increased, the total amount that may be depreciated is increased.

T F 17. An investment's cash flow is unaffected by the use of accelerated depreciation.

T F 18. If a firm uses straight-line depreciation instead of accelerated depreciation, it writes off less of the asset's cost than if accelerated depreciation had been used.

T F 19. Depreciation is a source of cash flow because it increases a firm's earnings.

T F 20. The federal government encourages investment in plant and equipment by permitting firms to use accelerated depreciation.

T F 21. Some long-term assets such as land are not depreciated.

T F 22. If a corporation operates at a loss, the loss is carried forward to offset income in future years.

T F 23. The carrying back of operating losses by firms applies to both corporations and partnerships.

T F 24. Losses caused by accelerated depreciation expense do not receive the benefit of the carry-back and carry-forward provisions for loses.

MULTIPLE CHOICE

1. Most businesses are classified as
   a. sole proprietorships
   b. partnerships
   c. corporations
   d. trusts

2. A partner may not be liable for
   a. the creditor's debts
   b. the firm's debts
   c. personal debts
   d. the debts of partners

3. A tax is regressive if, as one's income rises,
   a. the tax rate increases
   b. the tax rate decreases
   c. the tax paid increases
   d. the tax paid decreases

4. An advantage of incorporation is
   a. retained earnings are not taxed
   b. cash dividends
   c. ownership may be easily transferred
   d. stockholders have unlimited liability

5. The federal corporate income tax
   a. is decreased by the distribution of earnings
   b. is increased by the distribution of earnings
   c. is decreased by depreciation
   d. is increased by depreciation

6. If investors anticipate reinvesting funds in a firm so it may grow, they will prefer which of the following business forms?
   a. sole proprietorships
   b. limited partnerships
   c. corporations
   d. S corporations

7. Cash flow is equal to
   a. earnings
   b. earnings plus interest
   c. earnings before interest and taxes
   d. earnings plus deprecation

8. Which of the following is true concerning depreciation expense?
   1. allocates the cost of an investment over a period of time
   2. reduces the firm's interest expense
   3. is decreased by the investment's salvage value
   4. decreases the firm's income taxes
      a. 1 and 3
      b. 1 and 4
      c. 2 and 3
      d. 2 and 4

9. Straight-line depreciation
   1. is less advantageous than accelerated depreciation
   2. is more advantageous than accelerated depreciation
   3. reduces the cost of an investment by the same proportion each year
   4. reduces the cost of an investment by the same amount each year
      a. 1 and 3
      b. 1 and 4
      c. 2 and 3
      d. 2 and 4

10. Accelerated deprecation is beneficial to a firm because
    a. it initially increases an investment's cash flow
    b. it initially increases earnings
    c. it reduces the firm's expenses
    d. it reduces the firm's liabilities

11. No matter which method of depreciation is used,
    a. the firm's earnings are not initially affected
    b. the firm's cash flow is not affected
    c. the total amount depreciated does not exceed the asset's cost
    d. the total amount depreciated does not exceed the asset's replacement cost

12. Depreciation applies to investments in
    a. land
    b. equipment
    c. certificates of deposit
    d. corporate stock

13. Corporate operating losses are
    a. carried forward up to fifteen years
    b. carried back up to three years
    c. carried forward fifteen years and then back three years
    d. carried back three years and then forward fifteen years

14. Which of the following increases a firm's cash flow?
    a. interest
    b. operating losses
    c. depreciation
    d. investments in land

ANSWERS TO FILL IN THE BLANKS

 1. sole proprietorships, partnerships, corporations
 2. ownership (title), incorporating, limited
 3. state, bylaws
 4. progressive
 5. S corporation
 6. unlimited
 7. marginal
 8. capital
 9. depreciation
10. accelerated, straight-line
11. earnings, taxes
12. added
13. six months
14. three years, fifteen years
15. refund

Chapter 16
ANALYSIS OF FINANCIAL STATEMENTS

I. General Accounting Principles
   A. Reliable
   B. Understandable
   C. Comparable

II. The Balance Sheet
   A. Assets
      1. Current: cash, accounts receivable, inventory
      2. Long-term: land, plant, and equipment
      3. Investments
   B. Liabilities
      1. Current: accounts and notes payable, accruals
      2. Long-term: bonds
      3. Deferred taxes
   C. Equity
      1. Common stock and paid-in capital
      2. Retained earnings
      3. Treasury stock
   D. Book values versus market values

III. The Income Statement
   A. Determination of profit or loss
   B. Earnings per share
   C. Distribution or retention of earnings

IV. The Statement of Cash Flows
   A. Operating activities
   B. Investment activities
   C. Financing activities

V. Limitations of Accounting Data

VI. Ratio Analysis
   A. Classification of ratios
   B. Time series and cross sectional analysis

VII. Liquidity ratios
   A. Current ratio
   B. Limitations of the current ratio
   C. Quick ratio (acid test)
   D. The components of the current assets

VIII. Activity ratios
   A. Inventory turnover
   B. Receivables turnover and average collection period
   C. Fixed asset turnover
   D. Total asset turnover

IX. Profitability ratios
   A. Operating profit margin
   B. Net profit margin
   C. Gross profit margin
   D. Return on assets and return on equity
   E. Basic earning power

 X. Leverage ratios
   A. Debt/net worth
   B. Debt/total assets (the debt ratio)
   C. DuPont system of financial analysis

XI. Coverage ratios: times-interest-earned

XII. An Application of Ratio Analysis

SUMMARY

Financial statements are used by the financial manager (and creditors and investors) as a source of data to help make intelligent financial decisions. Financial statements should be reliable, understandable, and comparable.

The balance sheet enumerates at a point in time a firm's assets (what it owns), liabilities (what it owes), and equity (what the owners have invested in the firm). Assets and liabilities are classified as current (short-term or less than one year's duration) or long-term (more than one year).

The income statement shows the profits or losses of the firm over a period of time such as a year. It enumerates revenues and expenses to determine if the firm is generating earnings. Earnings are either retained or distributed.

The statement of cash flows places emphasis on isolating the capacity of the firm's ability to generate cash by its operations. The statement enumerates cash inflows and cash outflows and thus shows the sources of the firm's cash and how the cash was deployed over a period of time.

Accounting data has inherent weaknesses. The use of historical data automatically sets decision making into a time frame. Nonmeasurable items, such as the quality of management, may not be accounted for on financial statements. Valuation of assets using historical cost may understate an asset's value, and the impact of inflation is not reflected in the statements. By having financial statements audited by a CPA, a firm assures that the financial statements are presented in conformity with generally accepted accounting principles.

The use of ratios to analyze financial statements is frequently employed by financial managers, creditors, and investors. It may be used by management as a tool for planning or control, as a means to identify weaknesses in a firm, and as a device for comparing firms within a particular industry.

There are several general types of ratios. Liquidity ratios give an indication of the firm's ability to meet its debt obligations as they come due. Activity ratios determine how rapidly assets such as inventory and accounts receivable flow through the firm (i.e., are converted into cash). Profitability ratios measure performance. They show the profitability of a firm's operations are relative to some base such as sales, assets, or equity. Leverage ratios indicate how the firm is financed by identifying what proportion of the firm's assets were acquired through the use of debt financing. Coverage ratios indicate the ability of the firm to meet certain expense such as the coverage of the interest payment.

Ratio analysis may be used to compare firms within an industry (cross sectional analysis) or with itself over a period of time (time series analysis). The financial analyst should realize that industry averages may not employ the same definitions as those used by the analyst. It is important for the analyst to be aware of the ratio definitions employed and to be consistent in the application of the analysis. Without such consistency, the analysis may be biased.

FILL IN THE BLANKS

1. Current assets include _____, _____, and _____.

2. Total assets equals _____ plus _____.

3. An _____ is made for doubtful accounts.

4. Long-term debt is due after _____.

5. A balance sheet is constructed as of a _____ in time.

6. Earnings per share are _____ divided by _____.

7. Sales minus cost of goods sold and administrative expense is _____.

8. If a firm repurchases its own stock, it may hold the stock in _____.

9. An increase in an asset is a cash _____.

10. An increase in a liability is a cash _____.

11. A new issue of stock is a cash _____.

12. Distributing cash dividends is a cash _____.

13. If financing activities exceed operating activities plus long-term investments, the firm's cash position _____.

14. The credibility of financial statements is increased if they are _____.

15. Assets whose value has risen but which are carried on the balance sheet at cost are referred to as _____.

16. General accounting principles require that financial statements be _____, _____, and _____.

17. Accounting statements constructed during the 1980s may not be comparable to statements created during the 1990s due to _____.

18. The quick ratio (acid test) is an example of a _____.

19. Comparing firms in the same industry is a type of _____ analysis.

20. Inventory is _____ from the quick ratio.

21. The average collection period (i.e., days outstanding) measures _____.

22. To smooth out fluctuations, the inventory figures used to determine inventory turnover may be _____.

23. The extent to which a firm uses debt financing may be measured by the _____.

24. The return on equity is a measure of _____.

25. The higher the times-interest-earned, the safer should be _____.

26. The DuPont system of financial analysis combines _____, _____, and _____.

27. Basic earning power relates _____ to _____.

28. The calculation of times-interest-earned uses _____, while the returns on equity and assets use _____.

29. From a creditor's viewpoint, a high times-interest-earned is _____ while a high debt ratio is _____.

PROBLEMS

1. Construct a balance sheet from the following information.

Accrued interest payable	$4,000
Accumulated depreciation	30,000
Trade accounts payable	10,000
Retained earnings	86,000
Accrued wages	11,000
Work in process	5,000
Finished goods	30,000
Plant and equipment	100,000
Cash and marketable securities	10,000
Land	10,000
Accounts receivable	32,000
Allowance for doubtful accounts	2,000
Bank note (due in six months)	15,000
Long-term debt	15,000
Raw materials	7,000
Investments	10,000
Taxes due	1,000
Additional paid-in capital	20,000
$1 par value common stock 20,000 shares authorized 10,000 shares outstanding	

2. Determine a firm's earnings per share from the following information.

Corporate income tax rate	25%
Number of shares outstanding	10,000
Cost of goods sold	$60,000
Interest earned	2,400
Selling and administrative expense	15,000
Interest expense	5,000
Sales	100,000
Annual credit sales	90,000

3. Given the following information, construct the statement of cash flows. What happened to the firm's liquidity position during the year?

Net income	$16.7
Decrease in accounts receivable	6.1
Increase in accounts payable	13.6
Sale of bonds	55.1
Dividends	14.8
Retirement of bonds	10.8
Increase in inventory	15.2
Depreciation expense	56.0

Cost of goods sold	72.1
Reduction in income taxes payable	5.0
Sale of stock	0.4
Purchase of plant and equipment	91.0
Beginning cash	1.1
Repurchase of stock	5.6

4. Using the income statement and balance sheet constructed in (1) and (2), compute the following ratios. Compare the results with the industry averages. What strengths and weaknesses are apparent?

RATIO	INDUSTRY AVERAGE
Current ratio	2:1
Acid test (quick ratio)	1:1
Inventory turnover	
a. annual sales	2.5
b. cost of goods sold	1.2
Receivables turnover	
a. annual credit sales	5.0x
b. annual sales	6.0x
Average collection period	2.5 months
Operating profit margin	26%
Net profit margin	19%
Return on assets	10%
Return on equity	15%
Debt/equity	33%
Debt ratio (debt/total assets)	25%
Times-interest-earned	7.1x

Additional information:

last year's inventory	$40,000
credit sales	$90,000

TRUE/FALSE

T F 1. Paid-in capital is part of stockholders' equity in a firm.

T F 2. Issuing new stock or borrowing from a bank is a cash inflow.

T F 3. Since inventory may be held for more than one year, it is not a current asset.

T F 4. Retained earnings represent cash.

T F 5. An increase in accounts payable because they have to be repaid is a cash outflow.

T F 6. Assets plus equity equals liabilities.

T F 7. A balance sheet is constructed for a point in time.

T F 8. Long-term debt that matures in this fiscal year is
        classified as a current liability.

T F 9. The statement of cash flows indicates how the firm's
        assets generate cash.

T F 10. Since not all accounts receivable will be collected, the
        value given on the balance sheet is adjusted to allow for
        bad accounts.

T F 11. An income statement shows how much the firm earned and
        the cash generated during a period of time.

T F 12. Earnings per share tells investors how much dividends
        they will receive.

T F 13. Interest and dividends are paid before income taxes.

T F 14. The book value of the firm may not represent what the
        firm is worth.

T F 15. Inventory consists of raw materials, work-in-process, and
        finished goods.

T F 16. Current earnings that are retained cannot be distributed
        in the future as dividends.

T F 17. The statement of cash flows indicates the firm's cash
        inflows and outflows and shows the difference between
        cash at the beginning and end of the fiscal year.

T F 18. An increase in retained earnings is a cash inflow.

T F 19. Increases in both current assets and long-term investments
        represent cash inflows.

T F 20. Financial statements of publicly held firms must be
        audited by CPAs.

T F 21. The numerical value of the quick ratio cannot exceed the
        numerical value of the current ratio.

T F 22. If a firm has a large increase in sales near the end of
        its fiscal year, inventory turnover may be overstated.

T F 23. If the "times-interest-earned" were 1.5, that implies the
        interest payments will not be made.

T F 24. The acid test is better than the current ratio as a measure of liquidity for a furniture company.

T F 25. If accounts receivable are collected, the current ratio increases.

T F 26. If inventory is sold for cash, the quick ratio rises.

T F 27. Selling short-term government securities and using the funds to purchase inventory will reduce the current ratio.

T F 28. Selling short-term government securities and using the funds to purchase inventory will reduce the quick ratio.

T F 29. If a firm issues long-term debt and uses the proceeds to retire short-term debt, the current ratio is unaffected.

T F 30. Cross-sectional analysis refers to comparing firms over a period of time.

T F 31. Activity ratios seek to show how rapidly assets such as accounts receivable flow through the firm (i.e., are sold and generate cash).

T F 32. A rapid inventory turnover may imply lost sales resulting from the firm being out of an item.

T F 33. The more rapidly inventory turns over, the more finance the firm needs.

T F 34. Increases in income taxes reduce a firm's operating income.

T F 35. There may be several definitions of some ratios, and the analyst needs to be aware of the definitions being employed.

T F 36. Undercapitalized means the firm lacks debt financing.

T F 37. The return on equity is the return the firm earns on its retained earnings.

T F 38. The DuPont system combines the return on assets, the return on equity, and the coverage of interest.

T F 39. Leverage ratios indicate the extent to which the firm owns plant and equipment financed by debt.

T F 40. If a firm has a large amount of debt financing, it is highly financially leveraged.

T F 41. If the ratio of debt to assets is 50%, then the ratio of debt to equity is 1:1 (excluding deferred taxes).

MULTIPLE CHOICE

1. Current assets include
   a. plant
   b. inventory
   c. equipment
   d. paid-in capital

2. Current liabilities do not include
   a. short-term bank loans
   b. accrued interest
   c. accounts payable
   d. paid-in capital

3. Operating income does not consider
   a. depreciation
   b. cost of goods sold
   c. taxes paid
   d. salaries

4. Assets equal
   a. liabilities
   b. equity
   c. liabilities plus equity
   d. liabilities minus equity

5. Equity includes
   a. cash
   b. investments
   c. retained earnings
   d. assets

6. According to accountants, assets should be recorded at
   a. the selling price
   b. the market value
   c. the lower of market value or cost
   d. the cost of the asset

7. Determination of earnings (profits) requires knowing
   a. paid-in capital
   b. cash
   c. retained earnings
   d. depreciation

8. Which of the following is a cash outflow?
   a. a stock repurchase
   b. a decrease in inventory
   c. an increase in accounts payable
   d. a stock dividend

9. A new issue of bonds is
   1. a cash outflow
   2. a cash inflow
   3. a long-term asset
   4. a long-term liability
      a. 1 and 3
      b. 1 and 4
      c. 2 and 3
      d. 2 and 4

10. Which of the following is a cash inflow?
    a. an increase in cash
    b. a dividend payment
    c. a reduction in bonds outstanding
    d. a decrease in investments

11. Weaknesses in accounting data include
    1. undervalued assets
    2. non-measurable items
    3. historical instead of current replacement costs
       a. 1 and 2
       b. 1 and 3
       c. 2 and 3
       d. all three

12. The quick ratio (acid test)
    a. is unaffected by selling inventory at cost
    b. exceeds the current ratio
    c. is increased when long-term debt is retired
    d. is less than the current ratio

13. The current ratio is increased when stock is sold and the proceeds used to
    a. retire bonds
    b. purchase plant and equipment
    c. retire accounts payable
    d. pay cash dividends

14. An increase in inventory turnover may imply that
    a. sales are lower
    b. the price of the product has been reduced
    c. accounts receivable are collected faster
    d. the level of inventory has increased

15. If a firm collects its accounts receivable,
    a. the current ratio increases
    b. inventory turnover increases
    c. the average collection period is reduced
    d. inventory is reduced

16. Profitability ratios measure
    a. liquidity
    b. leverage
    c. performance
    d. turnover

17. The DuPont system of financial analysis combines
    a. profitability and turnover
    b. liquidity and turnover
    c. profitability and liquidity
    d. turnover and coverage

18. The higher the times-interest-earned
    a. the riskier is a debt issue
    b. the more subordinated the debt issue
    c. the safer are interest payments
    d. the smaller is the amount of outstanding debt

19. The more rapidly receivables turn over
    a. the more rapidly the firm is receiving cash
    b. the larger are the firm's sales
    c. the smaller is the firm's inventory
    d. the larger are the firm's accounts payable

20. The larger the debt ratio
    a. the more equity the firm is using
    b. the riskier the firm becomes
    c. the larger are the firm's total assets
    d. the smaller is the firm's use of financial leverage

21. The net profit margin
    a. is usually less than the operating profit margin
    b. exceeds the operating profit margin
    c. is not affect by taxes paid by the firm
    d. is reduced by interest earned

ANSWERS TO FILL IN THE BLANKS

    1. cash, accounts receivable, and inventory
    2. total liabilities, equity
    3. allowance
    4. one year
    5. moment (or point)
    6. earnings, shares outstanding
    7. operating income
    8. treasury
    9. outflow
   10. inflow
   11. inflow
   12. outflow

13. increases
14. audited
15. hidden assets
16. reliable, understandable, comparable
17. inflation
18. liquidity ratio
19. cross sectional
20. excluded
21. speed of collecting accounts receivable
22. averaged
23. debt ratio (or debt/net worth ratio)
24. performance (what the firm earns for its owners)
25. interest payments
26. turnover, profitability, leverage ratios
27. EBIT (operating income), total assets
28. operating income, net income
29. desirable (advantageous), undesirable

ANSWERS TO PROBLEMS

1.   Firm XYZ
    Balance Sheet for the Period Ending December 31, 19XX
    Assets
       Current assets
          Cash and marketable securities $10,000
          Accounts receivable $32,000
          Less allowance for doubtful
             accounts   (2,000)   30,000
          Inventory
             Finished goods   30,000
             Work in process   5,000
             Raw materials   7,000   42,000
          Total current assets $82,000

       Long-term assets
          Plant and equipment $100,000
             Less accumulated
                depreciation   (30,000)   70,000
             Land   10,000
          Total long-term assets $80,000

       Investments $ 10,000
       Total assets $172,000

Liabilities and Stockholders' Equity
    Current liabilities

Accounts payable	$10,000
Accrued wages	11,000
Bank notes	15,000
Accrued interest payable	4,000
Accrued taxes	1,000
Total current liabilities	$41,000
Long-term debt	$15,000
Total liabilities	$56,000

Stockholders' equity
    Common stock ($1 par value; 20,000
    shares authorized; 10,000 shares

outstanding)	$10,000
Paid-in capital	20,000
Retained earnings	86,000
Total stockholders' equity	$116,000

Total liabilities and stockholders' equity $172,000

2. Determination of the firm's earnings per share:

Sales	$100,000
Cost of goods sold	60,000
Gross profits on sales	40,000
Selling and administrative expenses	15,000
Operating income	25,000
Interest expense	5,000
Interest earned	2,400
Earnings before taxes	22,400
Taxes	5,600
Earnings available to stockholders	$16,800
Number of shares outstanding	10,000
Earnings per share	$1.68

3. Statement of Cash Flows for the Period Ending December 31, 19XX
    Operating activities

Net income	$16.7	
Depreciation	56.0	
Decrease in accounts receivable	6.1	
Increase in inventory	(15.2)	
Increase in accounts payable	13.6	
Decrease in income taxes payable	(5.0)	
Net cash provided by operating activities		$72.2

Investment activities		
Increase in plant	(91.0)	
Net cash used in investing activities		($91.0)

16-13

Financing activities
Proceeds from sale of long-term debt   55.1
Payments on long-term debt   (10.8)
Dividends   (14.8)
Repurchase of stock   (5.6)
Sale of stock   0.4
Net cash provided by financing activities $24.3

Cash at beginning of the year $1.1
Cash at the end of the year $6.6

The firm's cash position has increased, but that does not
mean the firm is more liquid since inventory and accounts
payable increased while accounts receivable declined. You
should also note that the firm increased its investment in
plant by using the cash generated through depreciation and
the issuing of new long-term debt. The earnings and sale of
stock did not cover dividends and stock repurchases. This
indicates that the firm is more financially leveraged.

4. Ratio analysis of financial statements:

Current ratio:
  Current assets/Current liabilities
  $82,000/$41,000 = 2

Acid test (quick ratio):
  (Current assets - inventory)/Current liabilities
  ($82,000 - 42,000)/$41,000 = .976

Inventory turnover:
  Sales/Average inventory
  $100,000/(($42,000 + 40,000)/2) = 2.4
or
  Cost of goods sold/Average inventory
  $60,000/[($42,000 + 40,000)/2] = 1.5

Receivables turnover:
  Annual credit sales/Accounts receivable
  $90,000/$30,000 = 3
or
  Annual sales/Accounts receivable
  $100,000/$30,000 = 3.3

Average collection period:
  Receivables/ Credit sales per day =
  $30,000/($90,000/365) = 122 days

Operating profit margin:
  Earnings before interest and taxes/Sales
  $25,000/$100,000 = 25%

Net profit margin:
  Earnings after taxes/Sales
  $16,800/$100,000 = 16.8\%$

Return on assets:
  Earnings after taxes/Assets
  $16,800/$172,000 = 9.8\%$

Return on equity:
  Earnings after taxes/Equity
  $16,800/$116,000 = 14.5\%$

Debt/Net worth ratio:
  $56,000/$116,000 = 48.3\%$

Debt ratio:
  Debt/Total assets
  $56,000/$172,000 = 32.6\%$

Times-interest earned:
  Earnings before interest and taxes/Interest
  $25,000/$5,000 = 5.0$

Times-interest earned (using net interest expense):
  Earnings before interest and taxes/Interest
  $25,000/(\$5,000 - 2,400) = 9.6$

Strengths: The current ratio, acid test, and inventory turnover are comparable to the industry averages. The operating profit margin exceeds the industry average. In general, the firm's financial performance is acceptable.

Weaknesses: There are two basic weaknesses. The first is the slow collection of accounts receivable which take 120 days to collect while the industry average is only 75 days. The firm is also using more financial leverage than the average firm as its debt ratio is 32.6 percent versus an industry average of 24 percent. This increased use of debt financing may be the result of carrying too many accounts receivable. If the firm were to collect its accounts receivable more rapidly, then it could retire some of its debt financing and reduce the debt ratio.

The increased use of debt financing could explain why the net profit margin is below the industry average. Since the operating profit margin is higher than the industry average, the lower net profit margin cannot be explained by the firm's operations. Either interest expense or higher taxes must be the source of the lower net profit margin. If the lower net profit margin is the result of higher interest expense, then this is probably the result of carrying too many accounts receivable.

Chapter 17
BREAK-EVEN ANALYSIS AND LEVERAGE

I. Break-even Analysis
   A. Total revenue: quantity times price
   B. Total costs: variable costs plus fixed costs
   C. The determination of the break-even level of output
   D. Uses for break-even analysis
      1. Changes in price or costs
      2. Substitution of fixed for variable costs
   E. Limitations of break-even analysis

II. Degree of Operating Leverage
   A. Measure of responsiveness of operating income to changes in output
   B. Equations to calculate the degree of operating leverage
   C. Substitution of fixed for variable costs increases operating leverage
   D. Operating leverage and risk
   E. Fluctuations in operating income
   F. Airlines and retailing compared

III. Financial Leverage
   A. Rate of return without using financial leverage
   B. Rate of return using financial leverage

IV. Financial Leverage and Risk
   A. Debt financing increases financial risk
   B. Increase in risk leads to higher interest rates
   C. Determination of after tax interest cost

V. Financial Leverage through Preferred Stock Financing
   A. Less risky to the firm than debt financing
   B. No tax advantage - dividends are not tax deductible

VI. The Degree of Financial Leverage

VII. Combined Financial and Operating Leverage

VIII. Leverage, Ratio Analysis, and Stock Valuation

SUMMARY

Break-even analysis is useful to the financial manager as it reveals the level of output at which the firm must operate in order to avoid losses. The break-even level of output depends on the level of sales (quantity sold and the price), fixed costs (those costs that remain constant regardless of the level of sales), and variable costs (those costs that vary directly with the level of sales).

The break-even level of output serves as a starting point for planning future expansion, changing the sales mix, or introducing a new product. It, however, does not indicate the profit maximizing or best level of production. Not does it indicate the level of output that maximizes the value of the firm.

The degree of operating leverage is a measure of the responsiveness of the firm's operating income (EBIT) to changes in output. Firms with large investments in fixed assets have a large degree of operating leverage. A larger proportion of their costs are fixed. Once these fixed expenses are met, earnings tend to rise rapidly with further increases in output.

Operating leverage increases business risk as the firm is obligated to meet its fixed expenses. The substitution of fixed for variable costs increases operating leverage and increases risk, as changes in output produce larger fluctuations in operating income. While operating earnings may generate higher earnings when the firm is expanding, profits will decline more rapidly if sales were to decline.

Financial leverage is the use of borrowed funds (that is, entering into fixed obligations such as interest) instead of the owners' funds. Successful use of financial leverage increases the return the owners will earn on their funds invested in the firm.

Borrowed funds must be repaid with interest. The financial manager will use borrowed funds only if the firm can expect to receive a higher return on the funds than the cost of the funds. Since interest is a tax deductible expense, the cost of borrowing is shared with the federal government through lower tax payments. This means the cost of debt is less than the stated rate of interest. This reduction in the effective cost of debt encourages the use of debt financing.

Preferred stock is also a source of financial leverage because the firm agrees to make a fixed dividend payment. However, the firm is under no legal obligation to make the dividend payments. Since preferred stock dividends are not legal obligations, the use of preferred stock is less risky than debt financing. The dividend payment is not tax deductible, which means the effective cost of preferred stock exceeds the effective cost of debt. Hence the tax laws encourage the use of debt financing instead of financing through preferred stock.

The degree of financial leverage is a measure of the responsiveness of earnings after interest expense to changes in operating income (EBIT). The fixed interest payment increases the volatility of earnings (i.e., increases the degree of financial leverage). Hence highly financially leveraged firms are riskier than less financially leveraged firms.

If a firm has a high degree of operating leverage, the financial manager should avoid using much debt financing. The combination of fixed interest expense with fixed operating expenses may unduly increase risk and reduce the value of the firm.

SUMMARY OF EQUATIONS

Total revenue:
(17.1) $TR = P \times Q$

Fixed costs:
(17.2) $FC = constant$

Variable costs:
(17.3) $VC = VQ$

Break-even: total revenues equal total costs
(17.4) $TR = TC$

Break-even level of output:

(17.5) $Q_B = FC/(P - V)$

Degree of operating leverage (DOL):

(17.6) $DOL = \dfrac{\text{percentage change in operating income}}{\text{percentage change in sales}}$

   or

(17.7) $DOL = \dfrac{Q(P - V)}{Q(P-V) - FC}$

Definitions of the symbols:
  P   price
  Q   quantity
  V   per unit variable costs

Illustrations:
   The price of a product is $5 per unit; the fixed costs of production are $300, and the variable per unit costs are $3. What is the break-even level of output? If output is 1,000 units, what is the degree of operating leverage at 1,000 units? What does that imply will happen to operating income if output rises 10 percent to 1,100 units?

Break-even level of output:
   $Q_B = \$300/(\$5-3) = 150$ units

Degree of operating leverage:

$$DOL = \frac{\dfrac{1,900 - 1,700}{1,700}}{\dfrac{1,100 - 1,000}{1,000}} = \frac{118}{100} = 1.18$$

or

$$DOL = \frac{1,000(5 - 3)}{1,000(5 - 3) - 300} = \frac{2,000}{2,000 - 300} = 1.18$$

The answers indicate that the firm must produce 150 units to break even. Production and sales of less than 150 units will generate a loss. The degree of operating leverage at 1,000 units is 1.18. This indicates that if output rises by 10 percent (e.g., from 1,000 to 1,100) the firm's operating income will rise by 11.8 percent. At 1,000 units of output, earnings are
  TR = 1,000 x $5 = $5,000
  TC = 1,000 x $3 + $300 = $3,300
  TR - TC = $1,700

At 1,100 units of output, earnings are
  TR = 1,100 x $5 = $5,500
  TC = 1,100 x $3 + $300 = $3,600
  TR - TC = $1,900

Thus when sales rose from 1,000 units to 1,100 units (i.e., a 10 percent increase), operating income rose from $1,700 to 1,900 (i.e., a 11.8 percent increase).

Cost of debt (k_d):
(17.8) $k_d = i(1 - T)$

Definition of the symbols:
  i   stated interest rate
  t   firm's marginal income tax rate

Illustration: If the coupon rate on a bond is 11 percent and the firm is in the 34 percent income tax bracket, what is the effective cost of the debt the firm pays?

Answer: $k_d = .11(1 - .34) = 7.26\%$

While the stated rate of interest is 11 percent, the effective rate is only 7.26 percent after the reduction in taxes associated with the deductibility of interest.

Degree of financial leverage (DFL)

(17.9) DFL = $\dfrac{\text{percentage change in net earnings}}{\text{percentage change in earnings before interest and taxes}}$

or

(17.10) DFL = $\dfrac{\text{EBIT}}{\text{EBIT} - \text{I}}$

Illustration: If EBIT is $1,000 and interest expense is $300 (i.e., EBT = $700), what is the degree of financial leverage if (as sales increase) EBIT rises to $1500 and net earnings rise to $1,200?

Answer:

$$\text{DOL} = \dfrac{\dfrac{1,200 - 700}{700}}{\dfrac{1,500 - 1,000}{1,000}} = \dfrac{714}{50} = 1.429$$

or

$$\text{DOL} = \dfrac{\$1,000}{\$1,000 - 300} = 1.429$$

These answers imply that a 10 percent increase in operating income generates a 14.29 percent increase in net earnings.

Total leverage

(17.11) Total leverage = degree of operating x degree of financial
leverage   leverage

Illustration: If the degree of operating leverage is 4 and the degree of financial leverage is 2, what is the total leverage?

Answer: 4 x 2 = 8

This implies that a 10 percent increase in sales will generate an 80 percent increase in earnings.

FILL IN THE BLANKS

1. Costs may be classified as _____ and _____.

2. The break-even level of output equates _____ and _____.

3. A measure of the responsiveness of operating income to changes in output is _____.

4. If a firm substitutes fixed costs for variable costs, the degree of operating leverage _____.

5. If the degree of operating leverage increases, the firm may become more _____.

6. Since a large proportion of an airline's cost of production are _____, the firm has a large _____.

7. Successful use of _____ will increase owners' return on their funds.

8. Financial leverage occurs when a firm uses _____ or _____ financing.

9. Interest expense is _____, but preferred stock dividends are not.

10. A measure of financial leverage is the _____.

11. The greater the degree of financial leverage, the _____ is the change in earnings to changes in operating income.

12. As the use of financial leverage increases, risk _____.

13. Total leverage is the product of _____ and _____.

PROBLEMS

1. The price of a product is $1 a unit. A firm can produce this good with variable costs of $.50 per unit and total fixed costs of $100.
    a. What is the break-even level of output?
    b. What is the break-even level of output if fixed costs were to increase to $180 but variable costs declined to $.40 per unit?
    c. What is the degree of operating leverage at 400 units before and after the change in costs?
    d. What are the implications of b and c?

2. Suppose the firm in the previous problem uses the initial cost
   structure and produces 400 units.
   a. What is the degree of financial leverage and total leverage
      if interest is $50?
   b. If sales increase 10 percent from 400 units to 440 units,
      what will be the percentage increase in total income?
   c. Confirm the percentage increases in operating income pre-
      dicted in questions 1. c and 2. b.

TRUE/FALSE

T F 1. If a firm has a high degree of operating leverage, it has
        few fixed expenses.

T F 2. Railroads have a higher degree of operating leverage than
        banks.

T F 3. If a firm's degree of operating leverage is 3.0, then a
        10 percent reduction in sales should decrease operating
        income by 30%.

T F 4. An increase in fixed costs (i.e., an increase in operating
        leverage) will tend to reduce risk since more of the firm's
        costs are known and cannot be changed.

T F 5. Increased operating leverage may be achieved by increasing
        variable costs relative to fixed costs.

T F 6. Break-even analysis does not show the level of output that
        maximizes the value of the firm.

T F 7. Linear break-even analysis assumes that variable costs rise
        with reductions in output.

T F 8. Total revenue equals price times quantity.

T F 9. Labor expenses are usually deemed to be a variable cost.

T F 10. The numerical value of the slope of the total cost schedule
        is 1.0.

T F 11. If a firm has fixed costs of $3,000, the price of its pro-
        duct is $4.00, and the per unit variable costs are $1.00,
        the break-even level of output is 1,000 units.

T F 12. The total revenue function TR = .5Q implies the price of
        the product is constant.

T F 13. If a firm has stable sales, a higher degree of operating
        leverage may be more acceptable.

T F 14. If variable costs exceed fixed costs, the firm is operating at a loss.

T F 15. One use for break-even analysis is to examine the effect of shifting variable costs to fixed costs.

T F 16. An increase in the debt ratio may be associated with an increase in risk.

T F 17. A firm would prefer to issue preferred stock instead of debt since it increases the degree of financial leverage.

T F 18. The fixed dividend paid by preferred stock is a source of financial leverage.

T F 19. If preferred stock paid a dividend that varied with the firm's earnings, preferred stock would not be a source of financial leverage.

T F 20. Since high use of financial leverage is associated with a lower degree of risk, higher financial leverage may also result in higher stock prices.

T F 21. Borrowing from insurance companies does not increase the use of financial leverage.

T F 22. The effect on earnings per share will be the same if a firm issues bonds with a 9 percent interest rate or preferred stock with a 9 percent dividend yield.

T F 23. A recession will cause earnings to fall more rapidly for less financially leveraged firms.

T F 24. If a company calls a bond and retires it, the use of financial leverage is reduced.

MULTIPLE CHOICE

1. Break-even analysis is not concerned with
   a. the relationship between financial leverage and risk
   b. the relationship between sales and profits
   c. the relationship between total costs and revenues
   d. the relationship between fixed costs and output

2. Variable costs
   a. are greater than fixed costs
   b. are greater than total costs
   c. are paid after fixed costs
   d. change with the level of output

3. To determine the break-even level of output, management must know
   1. fixed costs of operation
   2. per unit variable costs of output
   3. total sales
      a. 1 and 2
      b. 1 and 3
      c. 2 and 3
      d. all three

4. A union contract suggests that labor costs may be
   a. variable
   b. fixed
   c. a non-cash expense
   d. undetermined

5. If the firm substitutes fixed for variable costs,
   1. the use of financial leverage is increased
   2. the degree of operating leverage is increased
   3. the break-even level of output is reduced
   4. the business risk of the firm is increased
      a. 1 and 2
      b. 1 and 3
      c. 2 and 3
      d. 2 and 4

6. Straight-line break-even analysis implies that
   1. fixed costs eventually decline
   2. per unit variable cost may initially fall but start to increase with further increases in output
   3. per unit variable costs are constant
      a. 1 and 2
      b. 1 and 3
      c. 2 and 3
      d. only 3

7. If the degree of operating leverage increases,
   1. the firm has substituted variable for fixed costs
   2. the demand for the product has risen
   3. the element of risk may have increased
   4. the firm has substituted fixed for variable costs
      a. 1 and 2
      b. 1 and 3
      c. 2 and 4
      d. 3 and 4

8. Airlines have a high degree of operating leverage because of
   a. large investment in fixed assets
   b. small fixed expenses
   c. insufficient government regulation
   d. large use of debt financing

9. Business risk refers to
   1. use of accelerated depreciation
   2. the risk inherent in the nature of the business
   3. the sources of the firm's finances
      a. 1 and 2
      b. 1 and 3
      c. 2 and 3
      d. only 2

10. A high degree of operating leverage implies that
    a. earnings will not fluctuate as sales vary
    b. a small decline in sales will produce a large increase in operating income
    c. a large decline in sales will produce a small decline in operating income
    d. a small decline in sales will produce a large decline in operating income

11. Which of the following involves a fixed payment?
    1. bonds
    2. preferred stock
    3. common stock
       a. 1 and 2
       b. 1 and 3
       c. 2 and 3
       d. only 1

12. A firm may obtain financial leverage by issuing
    1. bonds
    2. preferred stock
    3. common stock
    4. retained earnings
       a. 1 and 2
       b. 1 and 3
       c. 2 and 4
       d. 3 and 4

13. Successful use of financial leverage may
    1. increase the firm's earnings per share
    2. decrease the firm's earnings per share
    3. increase investors' return on their funds
    4. decrease investors' return on their funds
       a. 1 and 3
       b. 1 and 4
       c. 2 and 3
       d. 2 and 4

14. The higher the debt ratio,
   a. the lower is the use of financial leverage
   b. the greater is the use of financial leverage
   c. the lower are the firm's total assets
   d. the greater are the firm's total assets

15. The increased use of financial leverage may
   1. affect the firm's credit rating
   2. decrease risk
   3. alter the firm's earnings
      a. 1 and 2
      b. 1 and 3
      c. 2 and 3
      d. 1, 2, and 3

ANSWERS TO FILL IN THE BLANKS

1. fixed, variable
2. total revenues, total costs
3. degree of operating leverage
4. increases
5. risky
6. fixed, degree of operating leverage
7. financial leverage
8. debt, preferred stock
9. tax deductible
10. debt ratio (or degree of financial leverage)
11. larger (more volatile)
12. increases
13. degree of operating leverage, degree of financial leverage

ANSWERS TO PROBLEMS

1. a. break-even level of output: $100/($1 - $0.50) = 200 units

   b. break-even level of output: $180/($1 - $0.40) = 300 units

   c. degree of operating leverage at Q = 400 units before change in costs:

   $$\text{DOL} = \frac{400(\$1.00 - \$0.50)}{400(\$1 - \$0.50) - \$100} = 2$$

   degree of operating leverage at Q = 400 units after change in costs:

   $$\text{DOL} = \frac{400(\$1.00 - \$0.40)}{400(\$1 - \$0.40) - \$180} = 4$$

d. This problem illustrates the effect of an increase in operating leverage. The firm must now produce more in order to break even. However, once the firm does break even, each additional unit of sales contributes more to earnings (i.e., the contribution margin of each unit of sales is larger). Before the substitution of fixed costs for variable costs, the firm broke even at 200 units of output; now it must achieve sales of 300 units.

The degree of operating leverage at 400 units of output has increased from 2 to 4. This indicates that a 10 percent increase in sales now generates a 40 percent increase in operating income while previously only a 20 percent increase would have occurred.

2. a. Operating income: $1(400) - $0.50(400) - $100 = $100

Degree of financial leverage:

$$\frac{\$100}{\$100 - \$50} = 2.0$$

Degree of total leverage:

$$\frac{400(\$1.00 - \$.50)}{400(\$1.00 - \$0.50) - \$100 - \$50} = 4.0$$

or

Degree of operating leverage x degree of financial leverage
= 2.0 x 2.0 = 4.0

b. The increase in operating earnings for a 10 percent increase in sales from 400 units to 440 units should be 20 percent (10% x the degree of operating leverage).

The increase in total earnings for a 10 percent increase in sales should be 40 percent (10% x the degree of total leverage).

c. Verification:
Earnings at sales of 400 units:
Revenues: $1.00(400) = $400
Expenses: $0.50(400) = $200
Operating income: $400 - 200 - 100 = $100
Interest expense: $50
Net earnings: $400 - 200 - 100 - 50 = $50

Earnings at sales of 440 units:
   Revenues: $1.00(440) = $440
   Expenses: $0.50(440) = $220
   Operating income: $440 - 220 - 100 = $120
   Interest expense: $50
   Net earnings: $440 - 220 - 100 - 50 = $70

Operating earnings rose from $100 to $120 for a
20 percent increase.

Net earnings rose form $50 to $70 for a
40 percent increase.

These percentages are the expected percentage changes in
part 2. b.

Chapter 18
PLANNING: FORECASTING AND BUDGETING

I. Planning
   A. A process of identifying goals and courses of action
   B. Financial plans within the strategic plans of the firm

II. Fluctuations in Asset Requirements
   A. Some assets vary with the level of sales
   B. Increments in some assets occur only if a particular level of sales is reached

III. Forecasting External Financial Requirements: Percent of Sales
   A. Assets and liabilities expressed as a percentage of sales
   B. Identifying assets and liabilities that spontaneously change with the level of sales
   C. Using the percentage to forecast assets and liabilities
   D. Constructing pro forma balance sheets

IV. Forecasting External Financial Requirements: Regression Analysis
   A. Simple linear regression estimates the following equation: $Y = a + bX$
   B. Using the estimated equation to forecast and construct pro forma balance sheets
   C. Regression analysis may increase accuracy of forecasts

V. Forecasting External Financial Requirements: Changes in Fixed Assets
   A. Output beyond capacity will required additional plant and equipment
   B. Relaxing the assumptions used in percent of sales

VI. The Cash Budget
   A. Budgets are planning tools
   B. Estimates of receipts and disbursements
   C. Cash budgets determine the flow of cash into and out of the firm
   D. Cash budgets determine when the firm will need short-term sources of finance
   E. Cash budgets determine when the firm will have excess cash which may be invested to earn interest

SUMMARY

Planning is the process of establishing goals and identifying courses of action or strategies. Financial planning is part of the overall planning of the firm and must fit in the context of the strategic plans of the firm.

Forecasting is used by the financial manager to plan for the financial needs of the firm. All assets must be financed. The financial manager must determine in advance which assets will be needed and when they will be needed, in order to plan for their financing. Such planning will facilitate obtaining financing as it helps identify when the firm will generate the funds to retire its debt obligations.

The percent of sales method and regression analysis are two forecasting techniques the financial manager may use. The percent of sales expresses those assets and liabilities, that spontaneously change with sales as a proportion of sales, and uses those percentages to estimate the future level of each asset and each liability that fluctuates with the level of sales. In order to make the forecasts, the technique assumes that the percentages will remain constant.

Regression analysis does not assume the percentage will remain constant. It estimates an equation that summarizes the relationship between assets and liabilities that vary with sales. Regression analysis tends to be more accurate than the percent of sales because it employs more information to determine its forecasts.

The forecasts obtained by the use of the percent of sales or regression analysis are used to construct pro forma (that is, projected) balance sheets. If projected assets exceed projected liabilities plus equity, the financial manager will have to plan additional financing in order to acquire the projected assets.

Budgets are tables estimating receipts and disbursements. They determine when the firm will have cash and when it will need cash. While budgets may be determined for any time period, the chapter illustrated the cash budget, which is usually constructed for a modest period of time such as six months. This budget is used by the financial manager to plan when the firm will need short-term external financing.

SUMMARY OF EQUATIONS

Inventory (I) or any asset or liability that spontaneously changes with sales (S):

(18.1) $I = bS$

Illustration:
  What is the level of inventory if inventory is 40% of sales and sales are $3,000?
    Answer: $I = .4(\$3,000) = \$1,200$

The determination of external funding requirement (EFR) using the percent of sales:

$$(18.2) \quad EFR = [\frac{A}{S}(\Delta S) - \frac{L}{S}(\Delta S)] - (PS_1)R$$

The symbols are
  S   sales
  A   assets that spontaneously change with sales
  L   liabilities that spontaneously change with sales
  P   profit margin on sales
  R   proportion of earnings that are retained
(Notice that the equation uses only those assets and liabilities that spontaneously change with sales. All others are excluded.)

Illustration:

  Suppose a firm determines that 53% of its assets vary with sales and 20% of its liabilities vary with sales. Currently sales are $10,000 and the firm earns 4% after tax on its sales and retains all of its earnings. If sales rise to $11,000, will it need outside funding?

    Answer:
    EFR = .53($1,000) - .2($1,000) - .04($11,000)(1.0)
        = $530 - 200 - 440 = $530 - 640 = ($110)

  The firm's assets increase by $530; its liabilities expand by $200. This $200 and the addition to retained earnings ($440) generated by the total sales of $11,000 more than cover its needs for outside financing. If the firm had distributed half of its earnings as dividends (i.e., $220), the firm would have only $420 (i.e., $200 + $220) available to finance the expansion in assets and then would require outside financing.

The general linear equation relating inventory (or any other asset and liability) to sales:

$$(18.3) \quad I = a + bS$$

Illustration:

  What is the level of inventory if sales are $3,000 and the estimated regression equation relating inventory and sales is $I = \$100 + .35S$?

    Answer: $I = \$100 + .35(\$3,000) = \$1,150$

FILL IN THE BLANKS

1. The percent of sales method of forecasting assumes that the proportion of assets that spontaneously change with sales is _____.

2. Regression analysis estimates _____ that relates inventory and other assets or liabilities to _____.

3. If assets expand more than liabilities and the firm does not retain its earnings, the firm will need _____.

4. A cash budget is essentially a table relating _____ and _____.

5. Non-cash expenses like depreciation are _____ from the cash budget, but non-tax deductible payments like principal repayments are _____.

PROBLEMS

1. A financial manager needs to forecast the level of inventory. Currently inventory is 60 percent of sales, but a regression analysis indicates the following relationship between sales and inventory:
   $$I = \$1,000 + .5S$$
   If the anticipated level of sales is $20,000, what is the level of inventory forecasted by (a) the percent of sales and (b) the regression equation?

2. A firm with sales of $1000 has the following balance sheet.

Corporation XYZ
Balance Sheet as of June 30, 19XX

Assets		Liabilities and Equity	
Accounts receivable	$200	Accounts payable	$200
Inventory	400	Long-term debt	300
Plant	400	Equity	500
	$,1000		$,1000

If the firm earns 10 percent after taxes on sales and pays no dividends,
a. determine the entries for a new balance sheet for sales of $1,500 using the percent of sales method of forecasting.
b. Will the firm need external financing?
c. Construct a new balance sheet using the estimates obtained in a. If necessary, issue new stock to cover any external financing needs. If the firm has excess funds, retire the accounts payable.

3. Prepare a monthly cash budget for a firm given the following information.

Sales:		
	June	$200,000
	July	200,000
	August	200,000
	September	300,000
	October	500,000
	November	200,000

70% of the sales are for credit and are collected one month after the sale.

Other receipts: $50,000 in October

Variable disbursements: 60% of sales each month

Other disbursements: $10,000 a month
  $80,000 for taxes in August
  $400,000 for debt repayment in November

Beginning cash: $50,000

Desired cash: $10,000

TRUE/FALSE

T F 1. Long-term liabilities vary spontaneously with sales.

T F 2. Accounts receivable are an example of an asset that may automatically vary with changes in sales.

T F 3. The percent of sales method of forecasting assumes the level of some assets varies proportionately with the level of sales.

T F 4. Plant and equipment spontaneously rises as the firm expands.

T F 5. Equity as a percent of sales is fixed.

T F 6. If accounts receivable are 15% of sales and sales double, the percent of sales method of forecasting says that accounts receivable will become 30% of sales.

T F 7. If profit margins increase as sales increase, the need for external finance is reduced.

T F 8. Regression analysis is limited to linear equations.

T F 9. Regression analysis may be used to estimate the relationship between accounts payable and sales.

T F 10. Regression analysis assumes that accounts receivable as a proportion of sales is constant.

T F 11. Budgets are useful for planning but not for control.

T F 12. If a cash budget shows that the firm will need funds in January and February, that indicates that the firm is operating at a loss.

T F 13. Rent is an example of an expense that is excluded from the cash budget.

T F 14. Non-cash expenses like depreciation are excluded from the cash budget.

T F 15. A cash budget is similar to an income statement because it includes sales and expenses.

MULTIPLE CHOICE

1. Which of the following assets do not spontaneously vary with the level of sales?
   1. accounts receivable
   2. equipment
   3. plant
      a. 1 and 2
      b. 1 and 3
      c. 2 and 3
      d. 1, 2, and 3

2. The percent of sales technique of forecasting assumes that
   a. inventory as a percent of sales declines as sales increases
   b. inventory as a percent of sales is fixed
   c. accounts payable as a percent of sales falls as sales increase
   d. accounts receivable as a percent of sales falls as sales increase

3. As a firm expands, which of the following is an automatic source of finance?
   a. long-term debt
   b. accounts payable
   c. mortgage loans
   d. bank loans

4. If a firm's sales increase by 50 percent and inventory was $100,000, according to the percent of sales method of forecasting inventory will be
   a. $100,000
   b. $120,000
   c. $150,000
   d. $175,000

5. Regression analysis assumes that
   1. inventory as a percent of sales may vary
   2. accounts receivable as a percent of sales may vary
   3. equipment as a percent of sales is fixed
      a. 1 and 2
      b. 1 and 3
      c. 2 and 3
      d. 1, 2, and 3

6. The cash budget excludes
   a. receipts
   b. disbursements
   c. tax payments
   d. depreciation

7. The cash budget includes
   1. tax payments
   2. accounts receivable
   3. principal repayments
      a. 1 and 2
      b. 1 and 3
      c. 2 and 3
      d. 1, 2, and 3

8. An estimated equation states that accounts payable equal
   $10,000 + .2 sales. If sales are $36,700, accounts payable are
   a. $15,340
   b. $17,340
   c. $19,240
   d. $21,040

9. Over-estimation of the required level of assets
   1. will cause the firm to acquire excess finance
   2. will reduce the firm's profitability
   3. will increase the firm's equity
      a. 1 and 2
      b. 1 and 3
      c. 2 and 3
      d. 1, 2, and 3

10. A cash budget differs from an income statement because the
    cash budget
    1. does not determine profits or losses
    2. includes taxes owed
    3. uses disbursements and not expenses
       a. 1 and 2
       b. 1 and 3
       c. 2 and 3
       d. 1, 2, and 3

ANSWERS TO FILL IN THE BLANKS

1. constant
3. external sources of finance
5. excluded, included

2. an equation, sales
4. receipts, disbursements

ANSWERS TO PROBLEMS

1. Percent of Sales:
   inventory = 60% of sales
   $$= .6(\$20,000)$$
   $$= \$12,000$$

   Regression analysis:
   inventory = $1,000 + .5(sales)
   $$= \$1,000 + .5(\$20,000)$$
   $$= \$11,000$$

   The regression estimate is $1,000 less than the percent of sales estimate.

2. a. Each asset (accounts receivable and inventory) and each liability (accounts payable) that spontaneously varies with sales increases by 50%. Since the firm earns 10% after tax on sales of $1,500 and pays no dividends, equity increases by $150. The new entries for the balance sheet are

accounts receivable	$300	+$100
inventory	600	+ 200
accounts payable	300	+ 100
equity	650	+ 150

   b. The expansion in assets exceeds the expansion in liabilities by $50, so the firm will additional external sources of finance. Possible sources include (1) a new loan from a commercial bank, (2) new long-term debt, or (3) new equity.

   The same conclusion that the firm will need $50 in external financing can be determined by the following equation:

   $$EFR = .6(\$500) - .2(\$500) - \$150 = \$50.$$

   c. If the firm issues new stock, its balance sheet becomes:

   ### Corporation XYZ
   #### Balance Sheet as of June 30, 19XX

Assets		Liabilities and Equity	
Accounts receivable	$ 300	Accounts payable	$300
Inventory	600	Long-term debt	300
Plant	400	Equity	700
	$1,300		$1,300

3. The cash budget shows that the firm needs cash during June. Once June has passed, the firm's cash position improves so the firm can easily retire any short-term loan taken out to cover June's cash shortage. The firm will also have sufficient cash to retire the debt that comes due in November.

Cash budget for	June	July	August
Receipts			
Sales	$200,000	$200,000	$200,000
Cash sales	60,000	60,000	60,000
Collections	--	140,000	140,000
Other receipts	--	--	--
Total receipts	60,000	200,000	200,000
Disbursements			
Variable disb.	120,000	120,000	120,000
Fixed disb.	10,000	10,000	10,000
Other disbursements	--	--	80,000
Total disbursements	130,000	130,000	210,000
Net change in cash	(70,000)	30,000	(10,000)
Initial cash position	50,000	(20,000)	50,000
Ending cash position	(20,000)	50,000	40,000
Desired level of cash	(10,000)	(10,000)	(10,000)
Excess (shortage) of cash	(30,000)	40,000	30,000

Cash budget for	September	October	November
Receipts			
Sales	$300,000	$500,000	$200,000
Cash sales	90,000	150,000	60,000
Collections	140,000	210,000	350,000
Other receipts	--	50,000	--
Total receipts	230,000	410,000	410,000
Disbursements			
Variable disb.	180,000	300,000	120,000
Fixed disb.	10,000	10,000	10,000
Other disbursements	--	--	400,000
Total disbursements	190,000	310,000	530,000
Net change in cash	40,000	100,000	(120,000)
Initial cash position	40,000	80,000	180,000
Ending cash position	80,000	180,000	60,000
Desired level of cash	(10,000)	(10,000)	(10,000)
Excess (shortage) of cash	70,000	170,000	50,000

CHAPTER 19
MANAGEMENT OF SHORT-TERM ASSETS

I. Working Capital and Its Management
   A. Working capital policy: management of current assets and current liabilities
   B. Net working capital: current assets minus current liabilities

II. The Impact of the Operating Cycle on Working Capital Policy
   A. Production process; the operating cycle
   B. Factors affecting the operating cycle

III. Financing and Working Capital Policy
   A. Short-term versus long-term financing
   B. Aggressive working capital policy

IV. The Inventory Cycle
   A. Inventory is acquired and subsequently sold
   B. Safety stock

V. The Economic Order Quantity
   A. Ordering costs
   B. Carrying costs
   C. Total costs
   D. The EOQ model
   E. EOQ illustrated
   F. Weaknesses in the EOQ model
   G. Maximum, minimum, and average inventory

VI. Inventory Valuation
   A. FIFO: first in, first out
   B. LIFO: last in, first out
   C. Impact on earnings and taxes
   D. LIFO - FIFO decision during inflation

VII. Management of Accounts Receivable
   A. Credit sales generate accounts receivable
   B. Credit policy
      1. Standards
      2. Collateral
      3. Terms of credit
      4. Importance of competition
   C. Analyzing accounts receivable
      1. Turnover ratios
      2. Aging schedules
   D. The decision to grant credit
      1. Additional sales
      2. Additional costs
      3. Incremental or change in net earnings

VIII. Cash Management
A. Cash management policies
1. Lockbox system of collections
2. Electronic funds transfers
B. Money market instruments
1. Treasury bills
2. Commercial paper
3. Negotiable certificates of deposit
4. Money market mutual funds
5. Repurchase agreements (REPOs)
6. Bankers' acceptances
7. Tax anticipation notes
8. Eurodollar certificates of deposit

IX. The Calculation of Yields
A. Discount yield
B. Annualized, compound yields

SUMMARY

The effective management of short-term assets (cash, accounts receivable, and inventory) is one of the most important tasks facing the financial manager. These current assets may be referred to as the firm's working capital. Since short-term assets must be financed, the financial manager must balance the cost of carrying these assets against lost sales from lacking sufficient inventory and from failing to offer credit. These assets may be finance by either short- or long-term sources of finance. The use of short-term sources is the more aggressive working capital policy. The cost of these sources tends to be less than the cost of long-term sources. Thus, the use of short-term funds may increase profits, but since these sources must be frequently refinanced, these sources are also riskier.

Inventory is acquired and subsequently sold. The larger the amount of inventory the firm acquires, the greater are the costs associated with carrying the inventory (such as the cost of finance and ware-housing). These costs may be reduced by carrying less inventory but this strategy will require more frequent orders, which also have costs (such as shipping, brokerage, and processing fees). One model used to balance these costs is the economic order quantity (EOQ), which determines the order size that minimizes the combined costs of carrying and processing inventory.

The EOQ model cannot assure that the firm will have inventory should sales occur more rapidly than expected or if inventory supplies were interrupted or delayed. To protect the firm from being out of stock, the financial manager may seek to maintain a minimum level of inventory, called a "safety stock."

If sales proceed as anticipated, the firm's maximum inventory is the EOQ plus the safety stock, and the minimum inventory is the safety stock.

Once inventory is sold, an accounting question arises as to which units of inventory were sold, the first ones acquired or the more recently acquired units of inventory. Under FIFO the "first" units "in" are considered to be the "first" units "out". Under LIFO the "last" units "in" are considered to be the "first" units "out". The use of LIFO during a period of inflation is prevalent since its use reduces the firm's current earnings and reduces income taxes.

Accounts receivable result from credit sales. Credit is offered to increase sales but the increased sales must be balanced against the cost of carrying these additional assets (i.e., the accounts receivable). These costs include the cost of finance, the collection costs associated with the accounts, and bad debt expense. If the firm decides to offer credit, it must establish credit standards, which determine who will be granted credit. In addition, the financial manager must determine the terms of credit and the firm's enforcement policy.

Accounts receivable may be analyzed through the use of turnover ratios (e.g., average collection period) or through aging schedules. An aging schedule is essentially a table enumerating what proportion of the firm's accounts receivable have been outstanding over various periods of time such as one or two months. These techniques enable the financial manager to identify weaknesses in the management of accounts receivable and which users of credit are slow payers.

Cash management policies are designed for speeding up collections, retarding disbursements, and investing excess short-term funds. A lockbox system may be designed to clear checks faster in order for the firm to have the use of the money more rapidly. Electronic funds transfer is a system of payment which immediately transfers funds to the firm when goods are sold.

Once the firm has made cash sales and collected its accounts receivable, the financial manager must manage the cash. While the financial manager could hold the cash and thereby be assured that the firm will have the funds to pay its liabilities as they come due, such a strategy does not generate income. Instead, the funds should be invested in money market instruments that pay interest and mature quickly.

Short-term money market instruments include Treasury bills (the short-term debt obligation of the federal government), commercial paper issued by credit-worthy corporations, negotiable certificates of deposit issued by banks, repurchase agreements, bankers' acceptances, tax anticipation notes, and Eurodollar certificates of deposit.

SUMMARY OF EQUATIONS

Total inventory costs = order costs + carry costs
  = (sales/size of each order)(cost per order) +
    (size of each order/2)(per unit carrying cost)

$$(19.3) \quad TC = (S/Q)F + (Q/2)C$$

Definitions of symbols:
  TC - total costs
  S - sales in units
  Q - quantity of inventory order
  F - fixed cost per order
  C - per-unit carrying costs

Illustration:
  What is the total inventory cost if

annual sales in units	100,000
number of orders	50
(2,000 units per order)	
cost per order	$5
per unit carrying costs	$1

Answer:
  Total costs = (100,000/2,000)($5) + (2,000/2)($1) = $1,250

Economic Order Quantity (EOQ):

$$(19.4) \quad EOQ = \sqrt{\frac{2SO}{C}}$$

Definitions of the symbols
  S - number of units sold during the year
  O - cost of placing an order
  C - per-unit cost of carrying the inventory

Illustration:
  What is the economic order quantity if annual sales are 10,000 units, the cost of placing an order is $1,000, and the per unit carrying costs are $100?

Answer:
  $$EOQ = \sqrt{\frac{2(10,000)(1,000)}{100}} = 447$$

Discount yield (y_d):

$$(19.5) \quad y_d = \frac{\text{Par value} - \text{price}}{\text{Par value}} \times \frac{360}{\text{Number of days to maturity}}$$

Simple (non-compound) yield (y_s):

(19.6) $y_s = \dfrac{\text{Interest earned}}{\text{Amount invested}} \times \dfrac{365}{\text{Number of days to maturity}}$

Illustrations: If you purchase a $10,000 short-term (ninety day) government security for $9,814, what is the discount yield and the simple yield?

Answer:
  Discount yield:

  $y_d = \dfrac{\$10,000 - 9,814}{\$10,000} \times \dfrac{360}{90} = 7.44\%$

  Simple (non-compound) yield (y_s):

  $y_s = \dfrac{\$186}{\$9,814} \times \dfrac{365}{90} = 7.69\%$

(The compounded yield is $(\$10,000/\$9,814)^{365/90} - 1 = 7.91\%$.)

FILL IN THE BLANKS

1. The difference between current assets and current liabilities is the firm's _____.

2. Holding excess cash costs the firm because it does not earn _____.

3. An increase in inventory financed by an increase in equity causes net working capital to _____.

4. During a period of inflation the use of LIFO instead of FIFO will result in _____ earnings.

5. The EOQ model combines the cost of _____ and _____ inventory.

6. The faster accounts receivable _____, the faster the firm receives cash.

7. One means to identify slow paying accounts is to construct an _____.

8. The desired minimum level of inventory is called the _____.

9. If the per unit order costs increase, the EOQ _____.

10. An increase in warehouse expense will _____ the EOQ.

11. Credit policy includes credit standards, _____, and _____.

12. The use of _____ reduces the risk associated with extending credit.

13. Excess cash should be invested in money market securities such as _____, _____, and _____.

14. Treasury bills are sold at a _____.

15. Treasury bills offer the advantages of _____ and _____.

16. The interest earned on tax anticipation notes is _____ from _____.

17. Bankers' acceptances are guaranteed by the issuing firm and _____.

18. If a firm sells a Treasury bill and agrees to buy it back, that is an example of a _____.

19. Negotiable certificates of deposit are issued in units of _____.

20. The yields on commercial paper are _____ the yields on Treasury bills.

21. Certificates of deposit issued abroad and denominated in dollars are called _____.

PROBLEMS

1. Given the following information, determine the economic order quantity and how often the firm will have to reorder.
   per unit cost of carrying inventory $5
   number of units sold annually   750
   cost of placing an order $100

2. Firm A uses LIFO, but Firm B uses FIFO. Both firms sell 100 units of inventory for $6,000. Each firm bought 60 units of inventory at $50 a unit on January 1 and 60 units at $60 on July 1. What is the difference in their earnings?

3. A firm has the following accounts receivable:

customer	amount owed	days outstanding
A	$1,000	15
B	530	32
C	680	45
D	1,050	18
E	115	63
F	320	22

If the firm's terms are n30, construct an aging schedule showing the percent of accounts that are one and two months overdue.

4. What is the discount yield, the simple yield, and the compound yield on a $10,000 nine month (270 day) treasury bill that cost $9,676? What are the same yields on a $10,000 six month (180 day) piece of commercial paper that cost $9,721?

TRUE/FALSE

T F 1. Net working capital is the difference between current assets and current liabilities.

T F 2. Increases in accounts payable and inventory suggests that net working capital also increased.

T F 3. The use of long-term sources of finance instead of short-term sources tends to decrease net earnings.

T F 4. If a firm uses short-term sources of finance instead of long-term, its financial risk is increased.

T F 5. The matching principle suggests that long-term assets should not be financed with short-term sources of finance.

T F 6. Rapid fluctuations in short-term interest rates is one source of risk associated with an aggressive working capital policy.

T F 7. Since cash is an asset, it is a source of finance.

T F 8. The safety stock is the minimum amount of inventory the firm seeks to carry.

T F 9. The economic order quantity is inversely related to the cost of placing an order.

T F 10. The economic order quantity is positively related to interest rates.

T F 11. The economic order quantity is inversely related to insurance and other carrying costs.

T F 12. According to the EOQ model, a doubling of sales doubles the desired level of inventory.

T F 13. LIFO is a method to depreciate inventory.

T F 14. FIFO refers to selling the first inventory received.

T F 15. During a period of inflation the use of FIFO instead of LIFO results in lower earnings.

T F 16. During a period of rising prices, the use of LIFO instead to FIFO results in lower taxes.

T F 17. Since the use of FIFO during a period of inflation reduces earnings, it raises taxes.

T F 18. Collecting accounts receivable increases a firm's current assets.

T F 19. Since accounts receivable may require an expenditure to collect, credit sales may reduce a firm's earnings.

T F 20. The more lenient the terms of credit, the riskier is the firm's credit policy.

T F 21. The purpose of aging accounts receivable is to identify rapid paying accounts.

T F 22. Credit policy requires the establishment of a collection procedure.

T F 23. Excess cash should be invested in long-term assets like bonds.

T F 24. Treasury bills do not pay a set rate of interest but are sold at a discount.

T F 25. Treasury bills and commercial paper are examples of liquid assets.

T F 26. A firm with $75,000 in excess cash may acquire a negotiable certificate of deposit.

T F 27. There are no tax-exempt money market instruments.

T F 28. A repurchase agreement occurs when a firm sells a Treasury bill and agrees to buy it back at a lower price.

MULTIPLE CHOICE

1. The matching principle suggests that
   1. equipment should be financed with long-term sources
   2. current assets may be financed with short-term sources
   3. plant should not be financed with short-term sources
      a. 1 and 2
      b. 1 and 3
      c. 2 and 3
      d. 1, 2, and 3

2. Which of the following increases net working capital?
   a. an increase in plant financed by retained earnings
   b. an increase in bonds and a decrease in equity
   c. an increase in cash and a decrease in accounts receivable
   d. an increase in preferred stock and a decrease in
      accounts payable

3. Which of the following increases financial risk?
   a. the substitution of equity for short-term debt
   b. the substitution of short-term debt for long-term debt
   c. the substitution of long-term debt for short-term debt
   d. the reduction of cash and marketable securities

4. The larger the interest rate, the larger is
   a. economic order quantity
   b. the number of units sold
   c. the cost of carrying inventory
   d. the firm's inventory

5. The economic order quantity is affected by
   1. the number of units sold during the year
   2. the safety stock
   3. the cost of carrying the inventory
      a. 1 and 2
      b. 1 and 3
      c. 2 and 3
      d. 1, 2, and 3

6. FIFO stands for
   a. first in, fast out
   b. fast in, fast out
   c. first in, first out
   d. fast in, first out

7. More stringent terms of credit will probably
   a. increase sales
   b. increase risk
   c. increase receivables turnover
   d. increase inventory turnover

8. The use of LIFO instead of FIFO during a period of inflation
   results in
   1. higher profits
   2. lower profits
   3. higher taxes
   4. lower taxes
      a. 1 and 3
      b. 1 and 4
      c. 2 and 3
      d. 2 and 4

9. Aging accounts receivable
   a. shows which accounts are slow payers
   b. requires a more lenient credit policy
   c. increases the firm's cash
   d. decreases the firm's inventory

10. Credit policy requires
    1. establishing the terms of credit
    2. determining to use LIFO or FIFO
    3. determining the collection policy
       a. 1 and 2
       b. 1 and 3
       c. 2 and 3
       d. 1, 2, and 3

11. If a firm has excess cash that it will need for a payment after
    three months, those funds should not be invested in
    a. commercial paper and repurchase agreements
    b. Treasury bills and treasury bonds
    c. negotiable certificates and Treasury bills
    d. bankers' acceptances and commercial paper

12. If a firm has excess cash that it will need after a period of
    four months, the financial manager may acquire
    1. negotiable certificates of deposit
    2. Treasury bills
    3. commercial paper
       a. 1 and 2
       b. 1 and 3
       c. 2 and 3
       d. 1, 2, and 3

13. The collection of cash may be increased by the use of
    1. a lockbox system
    2. electronic funds transfers
    3. aging schedules
       a. 1 and 2
       b. 1 and 3
       c. 2 and 3
       d. 1, 2, and 3

14. A lockbox system may increase the firm's profitability because it
    a. slows down the processing of checks
    b. retards disbursement of funds
    c. reduces the firm's float
    d. is a free service offered by banks

15. Which of the following will tend to increase earnings through increased sales?
    a. the use of a lockbox system
    b. the use of LIFO
    c. the extension of credit
    d. purchasing Treasury bills

16. Which of the following argues against extending credit?
    1. increased collection expense
    2. reduced collection expense
    3. increased bad debt expense
    4. reduced bad debt expense
        a. 1 and 3
        b. 1 and 4
        c. 2 and 3
        d. 2 and 4

17. If a firm has sales of $2,000,000 and does not offer credit but expects sales to rise to $2,500,000 if it offers customers thirty days to pay, which of the following will probably happen?
    1. receivables will turn over more rapidly
    2. receivables will turn over more slowly
    3. credit sales will increase by more than the increase in sales
    4. credit sales will increase by less than the increase in sales
        a. 1 and 3
        b. 1 and 4
        c. 2 and 3
        d. 2 and 4

ANSWERS TO FILL IN THE BLANKS

1. net working capital
2. interest
3. increase
4. lower
5. carrying, ordering
6. turn over (i.e., are collected)
7. aging schedule
8. safety stock
9. increases
10. decrease

11. terms, collection policy
12. collateral
13. possible answers: commercial paper, negotiable certificates of deposit, Treasury bills, bankers' acceptances, repurchase agreements, tax anticipation notes, money market mutual funds, Eurodollar CDs
14. discount
15. liquidity, safety
16. exempt, federal income taxation
17. the bank accepting (co-signing) the note
18. repurchase agreement
19. $100,000 or greater
20. greater than
21. Eurodollar CDs

ANSWERS TO PROBLEMS

1. $\text{EOQ} = \sqrt{\dfrac{2SO}{C}} = \sqrt{\dfrac{2(100)(750)}{5}} = 173$

The economic order quantity is 173 units. Since sales per day are approximately 2 units, (750/365), the firm will reorder about every 86 days (173/2).

2. Cost of goods sold: Firm A

60 units at $60 each	$3,600	
40 units at $50 each	2,000	
	$5,600	

Cost of goods sold: Firm B

60 units at $50 each	$3,000	
40 units at 60 each	2,400	
	$5,400	

Since the revenues were the same for both firms, ($6000), the difference in earnings ($400 for A versus $600 for B) is the result of the differences in cost of goods sold. Since firm A used LIFO, its costs were higher which reduces its earnings.

3. Aging Schedule:

days account:	0-30	31-60	61-90
A	$1,000		
B		$530	
C		680	
D	1,050		
E			$115
F	320		
totals:	$2,370	$1,210	$115

accounts receivable as percent of total accounts
0-30 days: 64.1%
31-60 days: 32.7%
61-90 days: 3.1%

Proportion of total accounts receivable that are overdue is
35.8 percent.

4. The yields on the Treasury bill:

   Discount yield:

   $$y_d = \frac{\$10,000 - 9,676}{\$10,000} \times \frac{360}{270} = 4.32\%$$

   Simple (non-compound) yield (y_s):

   $$y_s = \frac{\$324}{\$9,676} \times \frac{365}{270} = 4.53\%$$

   Compounded yield:

   $$(\$10,000/\$9,676)^{365/270} - 1 = 4.55\%.$$

   Discount yield:

   $$y_d = \frac{\$10,000 - 9,721}{\$10,000} \times \frac{360}{180} = 5.58\%$$

   Simple (non-compound) yield (y_s):

   $$y_s = \frac{\$279}{\$9,721} \times \frac{365}{180} = 5.82\%$$

   Compounded yield:

   $$(\$10,000/\$9,721)^{365/180} - 1 = 5.91\%.$$

I. Commercial Bank Loans
    A. Major source of short-term finance
    B. Loans are individually negotiated
    C. Credit lines
    D. Cost of commercial bank credit
        1. Prime rate
        2. Effective cost of a loan
        3. Compensating balances
        4. Commitment fees
        5. Installment loans

II. Trade Credit
    A. To finance inventory
    B. Spontaneous source of finance
    C. Effective interest rate
    D. Advantages of trade credit

III. Commercial Paper
    A. Unsecured promissory note
    B. Commercial paper ratings
    C. Types of paper
    D. Effective interest rate (cost of)

IV. Secured Loans
    A. Assets pledged
    B. Inventory loans
    C. Accounts receivable loans

V. Factoring

SUMMARY

Short-term assets may be acquired through the use of short-term financing from commercial banks, suppliers, issuing commercial paper, and other types of secured loans.

Commercial banks are a major source of short-term finance. Lines of credit and revolving credit may be obtained from commercial banks which give the borrower the option to borrow up to a specified amount of money. Such lines of credit provide the borrower with a flexible source of short-term funds.

Commercial banks charge their best customers the prime rate. They may increase the effective interest rate by requiring that the borrower maintain a compensating balance, by discounting the loans in advance (i.e., deducting the interest at the beginning of the loan), by requiring commitment fees, or by requiring installment payments. However, commercial bank loans may still be cheaper than other sources of short-term finance such as trade credit.

Trade credit is extended spontaneously by suppliers when goods are shipped on credit. Trade credit is a convenient source of finance that many small firms use because there are no other sources of finance available to them. The cost of the trade credit depends on any discount and the time period the borrower has the use of the funds. The effective cost will also depend upon the extent to which the borrower may ride the credit. Trade credit generated by terms such as 2/10, n30 tends to be more expensive than loans from commercial banks.

Commercial paper is unsecured short-term debt that is issued by large, credit-worthy corporations. The paper is either directly sold to the lender or placed through commercial paper dealers. Commercial paper is sold at a discount, and the larger the discount the greater is the effective interest cost of the paper. This interest cost is often less than the cost of short-term loans from commercial banks.

Firms may also use their assets as collateral to support short-term loans. Inventory and accounts receivable may be pledged to obtain short-term loans. Accounts receivable may be sold (i.e., factored) as another means to obtain short-term finance.

SUMMARY OF EQUATIONS

The simple annual interest rate (i_{CB}) on a commercial bank loan when the interest and principal are paid at maturity:

(20.1) $$i_{CB} = \frac{\text{interest paid}}{\substack{\text{proceeds of the loan} \\ \text{that the borrower} \\ \text{may use}}} \times \frac{12}{\substack{\text{number of months that} \\ \text{the borrower has the} \\ \text{use of the proceeds}}}$$

Illustration: What is the interest rate on a $1,000 loan for six months if the borrower pays $55 in interest at the maturity of the loan?

$$I_{CB} = \frac{\$55}{\$1,000} \times \frac{12}{6} = 11\%$$

The amount of a loan necessary to cover the desired funds plus the any compensating balance:

(20.2) $$\frac{\text{Funds needed}}{1.0 - \substack{\text{Compensating balance} \\ \text{required (as a decimal)}}}$$

Illustration: How much must a firm borrow if it needs $2,300,000 and the compensating balance requirement is 12 percent?

$$\frac{\$2,300,000}{1.0 - .12} = \$2,613,637$$

If the firm borrows $2,613,637, it will meet the compensating balance requirement (.12 x $2,613,637 = $313,636) and still have $2,300,000 to use.

Effective interest rate on an installment loan (i_{IL})

(20.3) $i_{IL} = \dfrac{2md}{P(n + 1)}$

Definitions of the symbols:
  m   number of pay periods in a year
  d   dollar amount of interest paid
  P   proceeds of the loan
  n   number of periods required for payment

Illustration: What is the effective interest rate on an installment loan for $500 with an interest payment of $50 if the loan must be paid off in six monthly installments?

$$i_{IL} = \frac{2(12)(50)}{500(6+1)} = 34.3\%$$

Cost of trade credit (i_{TC}):

(20.4) $i_{TC} = \dfrac{\text{percentage discount}}{100\% \text{ minus the percentage discount}} \times \dfrac{360}{\text{payment period minus the discount period}}$

Illustration: What is the cost of 3/20, n60?

$$i_{TC} = \frac{.03}{(1-.03)} \text{ times } \frac{360}{(60-20)} = 27.8\%$$

Effective compounded rate of interest on a discounted note:

(20.6) $i = (P_n/P_0)^{365/n} - 1$

Illustration: What is the effective rate of interest if $96,382 is borrowed and the borrower pays $100,000 after 95 days?

$$i = (\$100,000/\$96,382)^{365/95} - 1 = 15.2\%$$

Cost (simple rate of interest) of commercial paper (1_{CP})

(20.7) $i_{CP} = \dfrac{\text{interest}}{\text{proceeds used}} \times \dfrac{12}{\substack{\text{number of months paper} \\ \text{is outstanding}}}$

Illustration: What is the approximate, simple interest rate on a piece of $1,000,000 three month (i.e., 90 day) commercial paper that is sold for $987,654? What is the compounded, annual rate of interest?

$i_{CP} = \dfrac{\$12,346}{\$987,654} \times \dfrac{12}{3} = 5\%$

Effective, compound rate of interest:

$i = (\$100,000/\$987,654)^{365/90} - 1 = 5.17\%$

PROBLEMS

1. What is the cost (in percentages) of the following terms of trade credit?
    a. 2/20, n40
    b. 1/5, n30
    c. n30

2. A firm borrows $1,000,000 for a year from a commercial bank. The terms of the loan are 8% annual interest plus a 10% compensating balance. What is the annual interest rate?

3. A three month (90 day) piece of commercial paper is purchased for $97,500. What are the approximate and compounded yields on this investment?

4. What is the true rate of interest paid on a $5,000 loan with a finance charge of $1,400, if the loan is retired in 24 equal installments over two years?

FILL IN THE BLANKS

1. Commercial banks prefer to make _____ loans.

2. To increase the effective cost of a loan, banks may require _____ balances.

3. Discounting in advance _____ the effective cost of a loan.

4. _____ is credit extended by wholesalers to retailers.

5. The terms n30 means the firm must pay by the _____ day.

6. Generally the cost of trade credit _____ the cost of commercial bank loans.

7. The cost of trade credit varies with the _____ and _____.

8. Unsecured short-term promissory notes issued by large corporations are called _____.

9. Selling accounts receivable is _____.

10. If the discount on a loan increases, the effective rate of interest _____.

11. The amount that may be borrowed against inventory is _____ than the value of the inventory.

12. Commercial paper is sold at a _____.

13. If commercial paper is bought for a larger discount, the rate of interest earned _____.

14. If the terms of trade credit are changed from 2/20, n60 to 3/20, n60, the interest rate is _____.

15. The effective rate of interest on an installment loan depends on _____, _____, and _____.

16. Unlike a line of credit, a revolving credit agreement with a commercial bank is a legal _____ of the bank.

17. A blanket loan is secured by _____.

TRUE/FALSE

T F   1. Trade credit is cheaper than commercial bank loans.

T F   2. The larger the trade discount, the cheaper is trade credit.

T F   3. If suppliers want to discourage the use of trade credit, they may shorten the pay period (i.e., offer 2/10, n25 instead of 2/10, n30).

T F   4. An increase in the trade discount will discourage the use of trade credit.

T F   5. Trade credit is primarily used by retailers to finance accounts receivable.

T F 6. If goods cost $100 and the terms of credit are n30, the firm has 30 free days use of the goods.

T F 7. Trade credit may be used because it spontaneously increases as inventory increases.

T F 8. For many firms trade credit may be one of the few sources of credit available to them.

T F 9. A compensating balance, because it eases retirement of the loan, reduces the cost of credit.

T F 10. One method to increase the effective cost of a loan is to discount the interest in advance.

T F 11. Commercial paper is one source of short-term finance that is primarily only available to large corporations.

T F 12. The rate of interest that commercial banks charge their best customers is called the discount rate.

T F 13. The cost to a firm of a revolving credit loan is solely related to the firm's use of the credit.

T F 14. It is not wise to use a line of credit to finance the acquisition of plant.

T F 15. The interest rate on mortgage and installment loans is the true rate of interest.

T F 16. A firm cannot sell its accounts receivable at a premium to raise funds.

T F 17. Truth-in-lending legislation requires lenders to inform borrowers of the true interest rate.

T F 18. Commercial paper is primarily sold in small denominations of less than $10,000.

T F 19. When accounts receivable are sold to a factor, they are sold at discount.

T F 20. A loan secured by inventory may result in the goods being held in a warehouse owned by a third party.

T F 21. Blanket inventory loans are illustrations of unsecured short-term credit.

T F 22. The lower the reserve held by a factor the lower will be the cost of factoring.

MULTIPLE CHOICE

1. The rate of interest charged by a commercial bank
   a. is called the discount rate
   b. is generally lower than the rate on commercial paper
   c. is often stated as the prime rate plus some percentage
   d. is higher than the cost of trade credit

2. To determine the effective cost of a loan, the borrower needs to know
   a. the use of the proceeds
   b. the prime rate
   c. the length (or term) on the loan
   d. the margin requirement

3. Compensating balances
   1. generally increase the cost of a loan
   2. generally decrease the cost of a loan
   3. may be required by commercial banks
   4. may be required by suppliers
      a. 1 and 3
      b. 1 and 4
      c. 2 and 3
      d. 2 and 4

4. 2/10, n30 implies
   a. a 10% discount if the bill is paid in 30 days
   b. a 2% discount if the bill is paid in 30 days
   c. a 10% discount if the bill is paid in 10 days
   d. a 2% discount if the bill is paid in 10 days

5. The cost of trade credit will decrease if
   a. the discount increases
   b. the discount decreases
   c. the length of time decreases
   d. the firm increases its inventory

6. Trade credit may be used by a retailer because
   1. it is convenient and automatic
   2. it is an inexpensive means to finance inventory
   3. it is a suitable means to finance inventory
      a. 1 and 2
      b. 1 and 3
      c. 2 and 3
      d. 1, 2, and 3

7. Commercial paper is
   a. secured
   b. unsecured
   c. long-term debt
   d. sold in units of $1,000

8. Secured loans imply
   a. a specific asset supports the loan
   b. a specific account payable supports the loan
   c. the firm has little equity financing
   d. the lenders have little equity

9. Factoring is selling
   a. accounts receivable
   b. accounts payable
   c. commercial paper
   d. Treasury bills

10. Generally it is not wise to use
    a. long-term debt to finance long-term assets
    b. short-term debt to finance long-term assets
    c. long-term debt to finance short-term assets
    d. short-term debt to finance short-term assets

11. If a note is sold at a discount, the cost of credit does not depend on
    a. the amount of the discount
    b. the time to maturity
    c. the credit-worthiness of the firm
    d. the lender's profits

ANSWERS TO FILL IN THE BLANKS

1. short-term
2. compensating
3. increases
4. trade credit
5. thirtieth
6. exceeds
7. discount, difference between the pay period and the discount period
8. commercial paper
9. factoring
10. increases
11. less
12. discount
13. increases
14. increased
15. proceeds borrowed, dollar amount of interest, number of periods required for repayment and number of period in a year
16. obligation
17. inventory

ANSWERS TO PROBLEMS

1. Cost of trade credit (non-compound):

   a. $i_{TC} = \dfrac{.02}{(1 - .02)}$ times $\dfrac{360}{(40 - 20)}$ = 36.7%

   b. $i_{TC} = \dfrac{.01}{(1 - .01)}$ times $\dfrac{360}{(30 - 5)}$ = 14.5%

   c. $i_{TC} = \dfrac{.00}{(1 - .00)}$ times $\dfrac{360}{30}$ = 0.0%

2. The compensating balance is $100,000 ($1,000,000 x .1). Thus the amount of the loan that the firm can use is $900,000. The effective rate of interest is

$$\dfrac{\$80,000}{\$900,000} \times \dfrac{12}{12} = 8.9\%$$

3. The simple (non-compound) yield is

$$\dfrac{\$2,500}{\$97,500} \times \dfrac{12}{3} = 10.26\%$$

The compound yield is

$$i = (\$100,000/\$97,500)^{365/90} - 1 = 10.81\%$$

4. The rate of interest is

$$i_{IL} = \dfrac{2(12)(1,400)}{5,000(24+1)} = 26.88\%$$

Chapter 21
INTERMEDIATE-TERM DEBT AND LEASING

I. Intermediate-term Debt
   A. Five to ten year maturities
   B. Collateral and other covenants
   C. Repayment schedules

II. Leasing
   A. Contracts for the use of assets
      1. Operating leases
      2. Financial (capital) leases
   B. Classes of leases
      1. Direct lease
      2. Sale and leaseback
      3. Leveraged lease
   C. Lease versus purchase decision
   D. Accounting for leases
      1. "Off balance sheet" financing
      2. Capitalized leases
   E. Arguments for leasing
      1. Taxes
      2. Residual value
   F. Coverage of lease payments

SUMMARY

Term loans are intermediate-term debt of five to ten (and sometimes fifteen) years. These loans are usually collateralized by equipment acquired with the funds and retired through installment payments. In some cases the repayment schedules require a large lump payment at maturity (called a balloon payment). While commercial banks do make intermediate-term loans, insurance companies are the primary source of intermediate-term loans.

Notes are similar to term loans except they are sold to the general public, lack collateral, and usually may not be called prior to maturity.

Leasing is similar to renting. The _lessee_ has the use of the asset while the _lessor_ retains title (ownership). Operating leases include a maintenance clause and the lease may be canceled. These features are excluded from a financial lease. A financial lease is for the duration of the expected life of the asset and must be capitalized. The present value of the asset and the present value of the lease payments must be accounted for on the lessee's balance sheet.

Leasing may be an advantageous means to acquire the use of an asset, but the tax shelter associated with depreciation accrues to the lessor. In addition, since the lessor owns the asset, any residual value accrues to the lessor and not the lessee. If the lessor is in a higher tax bracket than the lessee, the tax code encourages the lessor to own and subsequently lease the asset to users whose tax bracket is lower. The terms of the lease may also be tailored to the mutual advantage of both the lessor and lessee.

The analysis of lease payments is similar to the analysis of interest payments. The lender (the lessor) is concerned with the ability of the borrower (the lessee) to service the debt (make the lease payment).

FILL IN THE BLANKS

1. Term loans are usually for _____ to _____ years.

2. Term loans are often secured by _____.

3. Term loans are often obtained from _____.

4. Term loans are generally paid off in _____.

5. Intermediate-term notes sold to the general public generally lack _____ and are paid off in their entirety at _____.

6. In a lease, the _____ owns the asset but the _____ has the use of the asset.

7. Types of leases include _____ and _____.

8. A financial lease is similar to _____ and must be _____ on the lessee's balance sheet.

9. If the lessor borrows funds to acquire an asset which the lessor subsequently leases out, that is illustrative of a _____.

10. Depreciation favors _____ over _____.

PROBLEMS

1. What is the repayment schedule for the first two years of a term loan for $100,000 for ten years with a rate of interest of 12 percent?

2. A firm could buy an asset for $20,000 by borrowing the funds at 10 percent for four years with interest paid annually and the entire loan repaid at maturity. The firm could lease the equipment for $5,800 a year including maintenance. If the firm does buy, maintenance will be $600 a year. The estimated after-tax salvage value is $1,250, and depreciation will be $5,000 annually. Construct projected cash outflows for each alternative for each year. Assume a 30 percent income tax rate. Is leasing the better alternative if the firm uses a cost of funds of 10 percent?

TRUE/FALSE

T F   1. All term loans are collateralized.

T F   2. Terms loans are often granted by insurance companies.

T F   3. Depreciation expense cannot exceed the annual repayment in a term loan.

T F   4. The lessee owns the asset while the lessor has the use of the asset.

T F   5. An operating lease usually includes a maintenance contract.

T F   6. If a firm sells a building and leases it back, that is illustrative of a leveraged lease.

T F   7. If a firm has a need for finance, it may sell an asset and lease it back.

T F   8. A firm's cash inflows and net income are the same under leasing or borrowing and purchasing.

T F   9. Leases must be capitalized (that is, accounted for on the firm's balance sheet).

T F 10. If a lease is capitalized, the liability is carried on the lessor's balance sheet.

T F 11. Leasing shifts the risk of obsolescence from the lessee to the lessor, but the lessee pays for this shifting of risk.

T F 12. If a lease is capitalized, both the firm's assets and liabilities are increased.

T F 13. If a lease is not capitalized, the firm's return on assets may be overstated.

T F 14. Both lease payments and depreciation are tax deductible expenses for the lessee.

MULTIPLE CHOICE

1. Term loans are usually
   1. for five to ten years
   2. unsecured
   3. for greater than ten years
   4. collateralized
      a. 1 and 2
      b. 1 and 4
      c. 2 and 3
      d. 3 and 4

2. Features of a term loan include
   1. restrictive covenants
   2. repayment schedules
   3. dividend payments
      a. 1 and 2
      b. 1 and 3
      c. 2 and 3
      d. only 2

3. If a term loan requires equal annual payments that retire the loan and pay the interest, that is similar to
   a. lease payments
   b. mortgage payments
   c. dividend payments
   d. a sinking fund

4. If a firm leases instead of borrowing, it
   1. owns the asset
   2. has the use of the asset
   3. receives the depreciation expense
   4. losses the asset's residual value
      a. 1 and 2
      b. 1 and 3
      c. 2 and 3
      d. 2 and 4

5. A financial lease is similar to an operating lease because
   a. it is cancelable
   b. it involves a maintenance contract
   c. the lessee owns the asset
   d. the lessor owns the asset

6. A firm may choose to lease if
   a. it is in a lower tax bracket and cannot use the depreciation expense
   b. it depreciates the asset
   c. the present value of its cash outflows under leasing are larger
   d. the asset's residual value is large

7. Many leases must be capitalized (i.e., accounted for on the firm's balance sheet) because
   a. the firm deducts the lease payments
   b. the effect of the lease is the same as borrowing and owning
   c. the firm has the use of the asset
   d. the lessee receives the benefit of depreciation

8. If a lease is not capitalized,
   1. the return on assets is overstated
   2. the return on assets is understated
   3. the use of financial leverage is overstated
   4. the use of financial leverage is understated
      a. 1 and 3
      b. 1 and 4
      c. 2 and 3
      d. 2 and 4

9. Capitalizing a lease
   a. reduces income
   b. reduces equity
   c. increases current assets
   d. increases debt

10. The risk of obsolescence is shifted to the lessee if
    a. interest rates rise
    b. interest rates fall
    c. technological change occurs faster than anticipated
    d. technological change occurs slower than anticipated

11. The advantages associated with leasing include
    a. accelerated depreciation
    b. capital gains of the salvage value
    c. deductibility of interest payments
    d. deductibility of lease payments

ANSWERS TO FILL IN THE BLANKS

1. five, ten
2. equipment or real estate
3. insurance companies
4. installments
5. collateral, maturity
6. lessor, lessee
7. operating leases, financial (capital) leases
8. long-term debt, capitalized
9. leveraged lease
10. owning, leasing

ANSWERS TO PROBLEMS

1. The annual payment:
   $100,000 = X(IFPVA 12%, 10y)
   X = $100,000/5.650 = $17,699

   Repayment schedule:

Year	Payment	Interest	Principal repayment	Balance owed
1	$17,699	$12,000	$5,699	$94,301
2	17,699	11,316	6,383	87,918

2. Determination of cash flows:

   Cash flows under purchasing and borrowing:

Year	1	2	3	4
Principal repayment	$ --	$ --	$ --	$20,000
Interest	2,000	2,000	2,000	2,000
Maintenance	600	600	600	600
Depreciation	5,000	5,000	5,000	5,000
Tax deductible expenses	7,600	7,600	7,600	7,600
Tax savings	(2,280)	(2,280)	(2,280)	(2,280)
Salvage value (after tax)				(1,250)
Cash outflows	320	320	320	19,070
Interest factor	.909	.826	.751	.683
PV of cash outflow	291	264	240	13,025

   Summation: $13,820

   Cash outflows under leasing:

Year	1 - 4
Lease payment	$5,800
Tax savings	(1,740)
Cash outflows	4,060

   Present value of cash outflows under leasing:
   $4,060(PVAIF 10%, 4y) = $4,060(3.170) = $12,870

   The present value of the cash outflows from leasing is smaller, so that alternative is to be preferred.

Chapter 22
COST OF CAPITAL

SUMMARY

Equity investors and creditors require compensation (that is, dividends, interest, or capital gains - price appreciation) in return for the use of their funds. This compensation is a cost to the firm that must be met when the firm makes investment decisions. In addition, these costs must be adjusted for taxes (if the expense is tax deductible) and flotation costs associated with issuing the securities. The financial manager must know these costs of funds in order to make investment decisions which use the funds. The return on an investment must exceed the cost of finance in order to increase the value of the firm. Thus determining the cost of capital and the best or optimal capital structure is one of the most crucial tasks facing the financial manager.

The cost of debt depends on the current rate of interest, the firm's income tax bracket, and the riskiness of the firm.

The cost of preferred stock depends on the dividend paid and the price of the shares. If additional shares are sold, the flotation costs, which reduce the net price to the firm selling the securities, must also be considered.

The cost of common equity is related to the dividend yield, the potential for growth, and the element of risk. The cost of retained earnings is less than the cost of new shares because selling new shares involves flotation costs.

The cost of capital for a firm is the weighted average of the costs of debt, preferred stock, and equity.

The correct balance among the various sources of funds is the firm's optimal capital structure. While debt financing is cheaper than equity financing, excessive use of debt financing increases risk. The financial manager needs to determine that combination of debt and equity financing that takes advantage of cheaper debt without excessively increasing risk. That combination minimizes the weighted average cost of capital and is the firm's optimal capital structure.

Even if the firm maintains the optimal capital structure, the cost of additional funds, the marginal cost of capital, may increase if the cost of any of the components rises. Such an increase may occur if the firm exhausts all of its internally generated funds (retained earnings) and must sell additional shares (with their flotation costs) to raise additional capital.

Maintaining the optimal capital structure should increase the value of the firm. There is a sophisticated financial theory that suggests that if financial markets were perfect, the value of the firm would not depend on the firm's capital structure. This theory helped justify the large use of debt financing in many leveraged buyouts and led to some firms actually having negative equity.

SUMMARY OF EQUATIONS

Cost of debt (k_d) [from Chapter 17]

(17.8) $k_d = i(1 - t)$

Cost of preferred stock (k_p)

(22.1) $k_p = D_p/P_p$

Cost of retained earnings (k_e)

(22.3) $k_e = \dfrac{D_0(1 + g)}{P} + g$

Cost of new shares (k_{ne})

(22.4) $k_{ne} = \dfrac{D_0(1 + g)}{P - F} + g$

Definitions of the symbols:
  i   the current rate of interest
  t   the firm's marginal tax rate
  D_p annual dividend paid by the preferred stock

  P_p current market price of the preferred stock

  D_0 current dividend paid by the common stock

  g   annual growth rate in the firm's earnings and dividends
  P   current market price of the common stock
  F   per share flotation costs

Illustration: What is the cost of debt, preferred stock, and retained earnings if
  i = 10%
  t = 30%
  g = 12%
  D_p = $1

  P_p = $10

  D_0 = $.50

  P = $12

Answers:
  k_d = $10(1 - .3) = .07 = 7%

  k_p = $1/$10 = 10%

  k_e = $\dfrac{\$.50(1 + .12)}{\$12}$ +   .12 =   16.7%

If the firm has exhausted its retained earnings and must issue additional shares, the cost of equity include flotation costs. If F = $1, the cost of new equity is

  k_{ne} = $\dfrac{\$.50(1 = .12)}{\$12 - \$1}$ +   .12 =   17.1%.

Weighted cost of capital (k)

(22.5) $k = w_1 k_d + w_2 k_p + w_3 k_e$

The only new symbol is the w which represents the weight of each source of funds in the firm's capital structure.

Illustration: What is the cost of capital if the firm uses 24 percent debt, 13 percent preferred stock, and 63 percent equity when the cost of each source is respectively 7 percent, 10 percent and 16.7 percent?

Answer:
  $k = (.24)(.07) + (.13)(.10) + (.63)(.167) = 12.04\%$

If the firm has limited funds available at a particular cost, then additional funds will cost more, which raises the marginal cost of capital even though the capital structure may be maintained. This increase in the cost of capital occurs after the firm has exhausted the cheaper funds. The point at which this break point occurs in the total amount invested is determined by the following equation:

(22.6) Break-point = $\dfrac{\text{Amount of funds available at a given cost}}{\text{Proportion of that component in the capital structure}}$

Illustration: A firm has $2,300,000 in retained earnings after which it will have to issue new shares; equity constitutes 40 percent in the firm's capital structure. After how much additional funding (debt plus equity financing) will the firm have to issue new shares?

Answer: $2,300,000/.4 = $5,750,000

After the firm raises $5,750,000 (i.e., $3,450,000 in debt and $2,300,000 in retained earnings), it will have to issue new shares as it will have exhausted the retained earnings.

FILL IN THE BLANKS

1. If a firm increases its use of debt financing, the rate of interest charged by creditors may _____.

2. The cost of debt is affected by _____, _____, and _____.

3. The cost of new equity exceeds the cost of retained earnings because of _____.

4. As a firm initially substitutes debt for equity financing, the cost of capital _____.

5. Preferred stock financing is more expensive than debt financing because _____.

6. In the capital asset pricing model, the cost of equity depends on the risk-free rate, the return on the market, and the _____.

7. If a firm earns more on an investment than its cost of capital, this extra accrues to _____.

8. The optimal capital structure _____ the weighted average cost of funds.

9. If the firm uses 20 percent debt financing and 80 percent equity financing, which cost 10 percent and 15 percent respectively, the firm's cost of capital is _____.

10. The cost of additional finance is the firm's _____.

PROBLEMS

1. Given the following information:

interest rate	8%
tax rate	30%
dividend	$1
price of the common stock	$50
growth rate of dividends	7%
debt ratio	40%

a. Determine the firm's cost of capital.

b. If the debt ratio rises to 50 percent and the cost of funds remains the same, what is the new cost of capital?

c. If the debt ratio rises to 60 percent, the interest rate rises to 9 percent, and the price of the stock falls to $30, what is the cost of capital? Why is this cost different?

2. Fill in the table using the following information.

Assets required for operation: $2,000

Case A - firm uses only equity financing
Case B - firm uses 30% debt with a 10% interest
        rate and 70% equity
Case C - firm uses 50% debt with a 12% interest
        rate and 50% equity

	A	B	C
Debt outstanding	$	$	$
Stockholders' equity			
Earnings before interest and taxes	300	300	300
Interest expense			
Earnings before taxes			
Taxes (40% of earnings)			
Net earnings			
Return on stockholders' investment	%	%	%

What happens to the rate of return on the stockholders'
investment as the amount of debt increases? Why did the
rate of interest increase in case C?

3. The firm's cost of debt is 8 percent, and the cost of retained
   earnings is 14 percent. However, if the firm exhausts its retained earnings of $23,678, the cost of equity rises to 14.9
   percent. Currently management believes that the firm's current
   combination of 35 percent debt and 65 percent equity is the
   optimal capital structure.
   a. What is the firm's cost of capital if it uses only retained
      earnings?
   b. What is the firm's cost of capital if it uses new equity?
   c. How much total financing may the firm have before the
      marginal cost of capital rises?

TRUE/FALSE

T F 1. The lower a firm's tax rate, the smaller is the incentive
        to use preferred stock instead of debt financing.

T F 2. The cost of preferred stock is greater than the cost of
        debt primarily as the result of the difference in tax
        treatment of dividends and interest.

T F 3. The cost of debt exceeds the cost of equity.

T F 4. Because interest is a tax deductible expense, the effec-
        tive cost of debt is less than the stated rate of interest.

T F   5. Preferred stock is infrequently used because it is more
          expensive than debt and offers no tax savings.

T F   6. Retained earnings are cheaper than issuing new stock
          because of the expense of selling the new shares.

T F   7. The weighted cost of capital includes the cost of all the
          components of a firm's capital structure.

T F   8. The higher the firm's tax rate, the more attractive is
          preferred stock financing.

T F   9. A firm can initially increase its use of debt financing
          without increasing the cost of debt.

T F 10. As a firm increases its use of debt, it becomes more
          financially leveraged and riskier.

T F 11. One technique used to measure the risk associated with
          preferred stock is its beta coefficient.

T F 12. The optimal capital structure is the firm's best
          combination of debt and equity funds.

T F 13. In order to maximize the value of the firm, the financial
          manager must determine the firm's optimal capital structure.

T F 14. The average cost of capital is the cost of additional
          financing.

T F 15. If the optimal capital structure has 60 percent debt
          financing, that suggests the firm should have $40 in debt
          for every $60 in equity.

T F 16. A firm cannot have negative equity.

T F 17. If a firm must issue debentures instead of equipment trust
          certificates, the marginal cost of capital may rise even
          though the optimal capital structure is maintained.

T F 18. If the marginal cost of capital rises, that suggests the
          cost of some component of the firm's capital structure has
          risen.

MULTIPLE CHOICE

1. The effective cost of debt is reduced because
     a. interest is a tax deductible expense
     b. interest is not a tax deducible expense
     c. interest is paid before preferred dividends
     d. interest is paid after common stock dividends

2. Preferred stock increases common stockholders' return
   a. more than an equal dollar amount of debt
   b. less than an equal dollar amount of debt
   c. more than an equal dollar amount of retained earnings
   d. less than an equal dollar amount of retained earnings

3. Debt financing is more risky for firms than preferred stock financing because
   a. preferred dividend payments are legal obligations
   b. interest payments are legal obligations
   c. preferred stock must be retired
   d. debt need not be refinanced

4. The use of financial leverage
   a. alters operating leverage
   b. magnifies the impact of changes in sales on operations
   c. moderates changes in net income relative to changes in revenues
   d. implies the volatility of net income is increased

5. The cost of capital includes
   1. cost of debt
   2. cost of preferred stock
   3. cost of retained earnings
      a. 1 and 2
      b. 1 and 3
      c. 2 and 3
      d. 1, 2, and 3

6. The cost of debt is affected by
   1. retained earnings
   2. firm's tax rate
   3. interest rate
      a. 1 and 2
      b. 1 and 3
      c. 2 and 3
      d. 1, 2, and 3

7. The cost of debt is
   a. less than the cost of equity
   b. greater than the cost of equity
   c. equal to the firm's interest rate
   d. greater than the cost of preferred stock

8. The cost of capital is
   a. greater than the cost of debt and equity
   b. greater than the cost of debt but less than the cost of equity
   c. less than the cost of debt and equity
   d. less than the cost of debt but greater than the cost of equity

9. Retained earnings
   a. have no cost
   b. are the firm's cheapest source of funds
   c. have the same cost as new shares of stock
   d. are cheaper than the cost of new shares

10. Flotation costs of issuing new securities
    a. decrease the cost of capital
    b. encourage the retention of earnings
    c. encourage external financing
    d. do not affect the cost of capital

11. The optimal capital structure involves
    a. minimizing the cost of all funds
    b. maximizing the cost of all funds
    c. minimizing the weighted average of the cost of funds
    d. maximizing the weighted average of the cost of funds

12. In the capital assets pricing model, the cost of equity is investors' required rate of return and includes
    1. the expected return on the market
    2. the firm's beta
    3. the firm's tax rate
       a. 1 and 2
       b. 1 and 3
       c. 2 and 3
       d. 1, 2, and 3

13. As a firm uses excessive amounts of debt financing,
    1. its debt ratio increases
    2. the value of its stock declines
    3. its cost of capital increases
       a. 1 and 2
       b. 1 and 3
       c. 2 and 3
       d. 1, 2, and 3

14. The marginal cost of capital
    a. is the firm's cost of debt and equity finance
    b. is constant once the optimal capital structure is determined
    c. declines as flotation cost alters equity financing
    d. refers to the cost of additional financing

15. Unless financial markets are perfect,
    a. the cost of capital cannot be minimized
    b. the optimal capital structure maximizes the value of the firm
    c. the marginal cost will exceed the average cost of capital
    d. using debt financing cannot increase the value of the firm

ANSWERS TO FILL IN THE BLANKS
 1. increase
 2. interest rate, tax rate, risk
 3. flotation costs
 4. declines
 5. dividends are not tax deductible
 6. beta coefficient
 7. the owners (common stockholders)
 8. minimizes
 9. 14 percent
10. marginal cost of capital

ANSWERS TO PROBLEMS

1. a. Cost of debt: $.08(1 - .3) = .056 = 5.6\%$
        Cost of equity: $\$1(1 + .07)/\$50 + .07 = 9.1\%$
        Cost of capital:
            weights x costs
               .4   x   .056   =   .0224
               .6   x   .091   =   .0546
                                      .0770 = 7.7%

   b. The cost of debt and equity are unchanged.
       Only the weights are changed.
       Cost of capital:
          weights x costs
             .5   x   .056 = .0280
             .5   x   .091 = .0455
                                .0735 = 7.35%

   c. Both the cost of debt and equity are changed.
       Cost of capital:
          weights x costs
             .6   x   .063 = .0378
             .4   x   .106 = .0424
                                .0802 = 8.02%

   The cost of capital changes as any of the components are
   changed. As the firm initially substitutes cheaper debt
   financing, the cost of capital declines (7.7% to 7.35%).
   However, as the firm uses more debt financing and becomes
   more financial leveraged, it becomes riskier, and the
   cost of capital rises (7.35% to 8.02%).

2.

	A	B	C
Debt outstanding	$ 0	$600	$1,000
Stockholders' equity	2,000	1,400	1,000
Earnings before interest and taxes	300	300	300
Interest expense	0	60	120
Earnings before taxes	300	240	180
Taxes (40% of earnings)	120	96	72
Net earnings	$180	$144	$108
Return on stockholders' investment	9%	10.3%	10.8%

The rate of return to stockholders rises because the after tax cost of debt in B is $.1(1 - .4) = 6\%$ and in C is $.12(1 - .4) = 7.2\%$. These costs are less than the 9 percent the firm earns after taxes on its assets ($180/$2,000). The interest rate increases because the firm becomes riskier when it uses more financial leverage.

3. a. The cost of capital using retained earnings:
$(.35)(.08) + (.65)(.14) = 11.9\%$

b. The cost of capital using new equity:
$(.35)(.08) + (.65)(.149) = 12.485\%$

(Notice that the marginal cost of capital rises after the firm exhausts its retained earnings and must start using more expensive new equity.)

c. The break-point in the marginal cost of capital schedule:
$23,678/.65 = $36,428

The retained earnings can support up to $36,428 in total financing and still maintain the optimal combination of debt and equity financing. However, after $36,428 of total financing, the retained earnings are exhausted, and the firm must start using more expensive new equity.

CHAPTER 23
CAPITAL BUDGETING

I. Valuation and Long-term Investment Decisions
   A. Identification of costs and cash outflows
   B. Determination of cash inflows

II. Payback Period
   A. Return of the cost of an investment
   B. Criticisms of the payback method

III. Introduction of Discounted Cash Flow Methods of Capital Budgeting

IV. Net Present Value
   A. Discounts cash inflows by the firm's cost of capital
   B. Net present value: present value of the cash inflow minus the present cost of the investment
   C. Acceptance criterion: net present value is equal to or greater than zero

V. Internal Rate of Return
   A. Equates the present value of the cash inflows and the cost of the investment
   B. Acceptance criterion: internal rate of return is equal to or greater than the firm's cost of capital

VI. Net Present Value and Internal Rate of Return Compared

VII. Using Financial Calculators to Determine Net Present Value and Internal Rate of Return

VIII. Ranking Investments
   A. Mutually exclusive investments
   B. Differences in the Timing of Cash Flows
   C. Differences in Cost

VIII. The Introduction of Risk into Capital Budgeting
   A. Using probability
   B. Risk premium added to cost of capital
   C. Use of beta coefficients and the capital asset pricing model

IX. Applications
   A. The replacement decision
   B. The refunding decision

SUMMARY

In order to select among competing long-term investment alternatives, the financial manager needs to apply the techniques of
capital budgeting: the payback period, the net present value, and
the internal rate of return. Each one requires identification of the
investment's cash outflows and inflows.

The most readily understood and easily computed method is the
payback period. The payback period is the number of years necessary
for the cash inflows to recoup the cost (i.e., the cash outflows) of
the investment. Investments with the shortest payback periods are
selected first.

The other methods of capital budgeting are more involved, but they
overcome the weaknesses associated with the payback period. Since
these techniques express future cash flows in present terms, these
methods are referred to as discounted cash flows techniques. The net
present value method discounts an investment's anticipated cash
inflows back to the present at the firm's cost of capital and sub-
tracts this amount from the present cost of making the investment.
If the net difference is negative, the investment should not be
made.

The internal rate of return method determines that discount factor
which equates the present value of the anticipated cash inflows with
the cost of making the investment. This unique discount factor is
called the internal rate of return. If this rate of return is
greater than or equal to the firm's cost of capital, then the
investment should be made.

Capital budgeting may be applied to many long-term investment
decisions such as selecting among competing uses for the firm's
funds, the replacement of existing equipment with new equipment, or
refunding a bond issue if interest rates have declined. Frequently
net present value and internal rate of return lead to the same
decisions. However, when there is reason to rank investments, the
two techniques may give conflicting rankings.

Ranking of investments is necessary when investments are mutually
exclusive (i.e., can make only one of the investments) or when the
firm has a given amount of funds and must ration the funds among the
possible investments. Conflicting signals between net present value
and internal rate of return may occur when the firm must rank
investments and the investments have differences in the timing of
their cash flows or differences in costs. Such conflicts require the
financial manager to explore other alternatives, especially the
reinvestment of the investment's cash flow, as a means to reconcile
the conflict.

Since all investments are not equally risky, it may be desirable to adjust for differences in risk. The cash inflows may be adjusted for the probability of their occurring with the standard deviation of the cash inflows as a measure of risk. Another technique applies the capital asset pricing model by using an investment's beta coefficient as a means to adjust for differences in risk.

SUMMARY OF EQUATIONS

Present value of an investment (PV):

(23.1) $$PV = \frac{R_1}{(1 + k)} + \ldots + \frac{R^n}{(1 + k)^n}$$

Net present value (NPV):

(23.2) $$NPV = PV - C$$

Internal rate of return:

(23.4) $$C = \frac{R_1}{(1 + r)} + \ldots + \frac{R^n}{(1 + r)^n}$$

Definitions of the symbols:

C   cost of the investment (cash outflow)
k   cost of capital
r   internal rate of return
$R_1 \ldots R_n$ cash flow in years 1 through n

Illustration: What is the net present value and internal rate of return for the following investment?

Cost (cash outflow) $1,000
Annual cash inflow   400
Life of the investment   5 years
Cost of capital   10%

Present value (PV):
$$PV = \frac{\$400}{(1 + .1)} + \ldots + \frac{400}{(1 + .1)^5}$$

Net present value (NPV):
$$NPV = PV - C = \$400(3.791) - 1,000 = \$516.40$$

(3.791 is the interest factor for the present value of an annuity at 10 percent for five years. In this illustration the net present value is positive, so the firm should make the investment.)

Internal rate of return (IRR):
$$C = \frac{\$400}{(1 + r)} + \ldots + \frac{400}{(1 + r)^5}$$

(If you do not have an electronic calculator that performs IRR calculations or a computer program, you will have to use interest tables. The use of tables is easy if the future payment is (1) a single amount or (2) an annuity.)

In this example, the five payments are equal, so the present value of an annuity table may be used. The equation collapses as follows:
$1,000 = $400(PVAIF x%, 5y)
   IF = $1,000/$400 = 2.5
   r is approximately 28% (28.65% using a computer)

The internal rate of return (28%) exceeds the firm's cost of capital (10%); hence the firm should make the investment. Notice that both the net present value and internal rate of return methods of capital budgeting conclude that the firm should make the investment.

FILL IN THE BLANKS

1. The period necessary to recover the cost of an investment is the _____.

2. Profits plus depreciation is _____.

3. The payback method does not consider the _____ of money.

4. Two discounted cash flow methods of capital budgeting are _____ and _____.

5. The net present value technique discounts the cash inflows by the firm's _____.

6. For an investment to be selected, its _____ present value must be _____.

7. The internal rate of return _____ the present value of the cash inflows and the _____ of an investment.

8. For an investment to be selected, its _____ must be equal to or exceed the firm's _____.

9. One method for adjusting for risk is to add a risk premium to the firm's _____.

10. If one investment alternative excludes another alternative, the investments are _____.

11. IRR and NPV may lead to conflicting decision concerning the selection of mutually exclusive investments if the _____ of their cash flows differ.

12. The _____ makes the more conservative assumption concerning reinvestment rates.

13. If an investment's cash flow increases, the net present value _____.

14. If the cost of an investment increases, the internal rate of return _____.

15. If the cost of capital increases, the net present value of an investment _____ but the internal rate of return _____.

16. The primary difference between the internal rate of return and net present value is the _____.

PROBLEMS

1. A firm has three investment opportunities. Each costs $1,000, and the firm's cost of capital is 10 percent. The cash inflow of each investment is as follows:

cash inflow	A	B	C
year			
1	$300	$500	$100
2	300	400	200
3	300	200	400
4	300	100	500

   a. If the net present value method is used, which investment(s) should the firm make?
   b. What is the internal rate of return of investment A? The internal rate of return of investment B is 10.22% and 6.15% for investment C. Which investment(s) should the firm make?
   c. What is the payback period for each investment?

2. A firm can buy new equipment for $10,000. It will last for five years, has no salvage value, and will save the firm $2,000 a year. The equipment to be replaced is carried on the balance sheet for $5,000. The old equipment can be sold for $5,000. Both the old and new equipment are depreciated on a straight-line basis. Should the firm replace the old equipment if its cost of capital is 10% and the firm is in the 40% income tax bracket?

3. Investments A and B are mutually exclusive and cost $2,000 each.
   The firm's cost of capital is 9%, and the investments' estimated
   cash inflows are

cash inflow year	A	B
1	$2,320	---
2	---	---
3	---	$2,810

   a. What investment(s) should the firm make according to net
      present value?
   b. What investment(s) should the firm make according to internal
      rate of return?
   c. If the firm can reinvest funds earned in year 1 at 10%, which
      investment(s) should the firm make?

TRUE/FALSE

T F 1. An increase in interest rates increases the net present
        value of an investment.

T F 2. An increase in investors' required rate of return will
        decrease the net present value of an investment.

T F 3. An increase in the cost of an investment will decrease its
        net present value.

T F 4. An increase in cash inflow that is not the result of an
        increase in profits has no effect on the net present value
        of an investment.

T F 5. The internal rate of return equates the net present value
        and the cost of an investment.

T F 6. If a firm's cost of capital declines, the firm will be less
        able to finance an investment.

T F 7. One weakness in the payback method of capital budgeting is
        that it fails to consider the time value of money.

T F 8. Since a firm can sell an investment's salvage value for
        cash, such value should not be considered when calculating
        the investment's internal rate of return.

T F 9. The prime advantage of the payback method is its
        simplicity.

T F 10. The net present value of an investment cannot be negative.

T F 11. Capital budgeting techniques may be used to aid in the decision to replace equipment before it wears out.

T F 12. The internal rate of return method of capital budgeting permits a ranking of investment proposals.

T F 13. The net present value can be adjusted for risk by adding a risk premium to the cost of capital.

T F 14. Even though an asset may still have useful life, it may increase the value of the firm to replace it.

T F 15. One of the factors that affects the decision to replace equipment is the firm's tax rate.

T F 16. If two investments are mutually exclusive, the firm can make only one of them.

T F 17. If the cost of capital rises, an investment's internal rate of return falls.

T F 18. If interest rates decline, the interest savings is insufficient evidence to refinance the debt.

T F 19. If a firm has only $1,000,000 to invest, it should buy the cheapest (least costly) investment.

T F 20. When selecting between mutually exclusive investments, the greater the reinvestment rate, the stronger is the argument to select the investment with the fastest cash inflows.

MULTIPLE CHOICE

1. If each investment costs $1,000 and has the following cash inflows, the payback method will select

year:	1	2	3	4
a. investment 1	$400	$300	$200	$100
b. investment 2	350	350	300	--
c. investment 3	300	300	300	300
d. investment 4	500	200	200	300

2. The payback method considers
   a. all the cash inflows from an investment
   b. the timing of cash inflows
   c. the cost of the investment
   d. the return on alternative investments

3. The net present value approach considers
   1. the cost of equity
   2. the cost of debt
   3. changes in current assets
      a. 1 and 2
      b. 1 and 3
      c. 2 and 3
      d. 1, 2, and 3

4. The internal rate of return will be higher if
   a. the cost of capital is lower
   b. the cost of the investment is higher
   c. the cost of the investment is lower
   d. the cost of capital is higher

5. The net present value will be larger if
   a. the cost of debt is higher
   b. any salvage value is omitted
   c. the cost of equity is lower
   d. depreciation expense is ignored

6. A firm should make an investment if the present value of
   the cash inflows is
   a. less than zero
   b. greater than zero
   c. less than the cost of the investment
   d. greater than the cost of the investment

7. A firm should not make an investment if the internal rate of
   return is
   a. greater than the cost of capital
   b. less than the cost of capital
   c. greater than the interest rate
   d. less than the interest rate

8. Risk may be incorporated into capital budgeting by
   a. raising the cost of the investment
   b. adjusting the cost of capital by a risk premium
   c. raising the internal rate of return
   d. lowering the cost of the investment

9. If an investment's net present value is negative,
   1. the firm should not make the investment
   2. the costs exceed the present value of the investment
   3. the investment will increase the value of the firm
      a. 1 and 2
      b. 1 and 3
      c. 2 and 3
      d. 1, 2, and 3

10. The replacement decision requires knowing
      1. the firm's cost of capital
      2. the cost of replacing the equipment
      3. the firm's tax rate
         a. 1 and 2
         b. 1 and 3
         c. 2 and 3
         d. 1, 2, and 3

11. If the net present value of two mutually exclusive investments
    is positive, the firm should
      a. make both investments
      b. make neither investment
      c. make the investment with the higher present value
      d. make the investment with the higher net present value

ANSWERS TO FILL IN THE BLANKS

   1. payback period
   2. cash flow
   3. time value
   4. net present value, internal rate of return
   5. cost of capital
   6. net, equal to or exceed $0
   7. equates, cost
   8. internal rate of return, cost of capital
   9. cost of capital
  10. mutually exclusive
  11. timing
  12. net present value
  13. increase
  14. decreases
  15. decreases, is unaffected
  16. discount factor

ANSWERS TO PROBLEMS

1. a. Net present value uses the cost of capital as the discount
      factor. First, discount the cash inflows by the cost of
      capital. For each investment that is

A	B
$300 x .909 = $272.70	$500 x .909 = $454.50
300 x .826 = 247.80	400 x .826 = 330.40
300 x .751 = 225.30	200 x .751 = 150.20
300 x .683 = 204.90	100 x .683 = 68.30
$950.70	$1,003.40

```
             C
$100 x .909 = $ 90.90
 200 x .826 =  165.20
 400 x .751 =  300.40
 500 x .683 =  341.50
               $898.00.
```

(Since investment A is an annuity, the present value could be determined by using the interest table for the present value of an annuity. That is
    $300 x 3.170 = $951
which is essentially the same answer except for rounding.)

Next subtract the cost from the present value to determine the net present value:

```
A:   $950.70 - $1,000 = ($49.30)
B: $1,003.40 - $1,000 =   $3.40
C:   $898.00 - $1,000 = ($102.00).
```

Since only B has a net present value that is positive, it is the only investment that covers the firm's cost of capital and hence is the only one that should be selected.

b. Internal rate of return for A:

$$\$1,000 = \frac{\$300}{(1 + r)} + \frac{300}{(1 + r)^2} + \frac{300}{(1 + r)^3} + \frac{300}{(1 + r)^4}$$

Since investment A is an annuity, the annuity table for the present value of an annuity may be used to solve the problem. Restated the equation is
    $1,000 = $300X
    X = $1,000/$300 = 3.33.

3.33 is the interest factor for the present value of an annuity for four years. Find this interest factor in the table to determine the internal rate of return. In this case the internal rate of return is approximately 8 percent, which is less than the firm's cost of capital. (The IRR is 7.7 percent if a financial calculator is employed). Therefore, the investment should not be made. (This answer is consistent with the answer given by the net present value in the previous question.) The internal rates of return for investments B and C were given. Only the internal rate of return of B exceeds the cost of capital; thus it is the only investment the firm should make.

c. The payback periods for the investments are
   A   three and one-third years
   B   two and one-half years
   C   three and two-thirds years.

   Notice that in this case the payback method gives the same ranking of investments as the net present value. However, the payback method does not tell if any of the investments should be made.

2. Increase in cash flow from savings $2,000
   Depreciation on new equipment $2,000
   Depreciation on old equipment   (1,000)
   Net increase in depreciation   1,000
   Income before tax   1,000
   Tax   400
   Net income after tax $600

   Net change in cash flow:
      earnings + depreciation = $600 + $1,000 = $1,600

   Cost of new equipment $10,000
   Proceeds from sale of old equipment   (5,000)
   Net cash outlay   5,000

   The change in the cash flow occurs for five years. The firm's cost of capital is 10 percent; the present value of the cash flow is
      $1,600 x 3.791 = $6,065.60

   The net present value is
      $6,065.60 - 5,000 = $1,065.60

   Since the net present value is positive, the firm should replace the old equipment.

3. a. Net present value of A:
         $2,320/(1 + .09) - 2,000 = $128

      Net present value of B:
         $2,810/(1 + .09)^3 - 2,000 = $170

      Since the investments are mutually exclusive, the firm cannot make both and will select B since it has the higher NPV.

b. Internal rate of return of A:
$$\$2,000 = \$2,320/(1 + r)$$
   PVIF = .862
   r = 16%

   Internal rate of return of B:
$$\$2,000 = \$2810/(1 + r)^3$$
   PVIF = .712
   r = 12%

   Since the investments are mutually exclusive, the firm cannot make both and will select A since it has the higher IRR.

c. There is an obvious conflict in the rankings. The purpose of this question is to help reconcile the conflict. If the $2,320 grow annually at 10 percent, then the future value is
$$\$2,320(1 + .1)^2 = \$2,320(1.210) = \$2,807.20$$

   Investment B is now clearly preferred to A because the terminal value of S is $2,807.20, which is less than $2810.

I. Mergers
   A. Reasons for external growth
   B. Possible impact on earnings per share
   C. Synergy
   D. Types of mergers: horizontal, vertical, and conglomerate

II. Executing the Merger
   A. Terms of a merger
   B. Means of payment
   C. The tax advantage of the stock swap

III. Pooling and Purchasing - Accounting for the Merger
   A. Pooling - a horizontal summation
   B. Purchasing - the establishment of a price
   C. Creation of goodwill

IV. The Hostile Takeover
   A. The initial offer
   B. Means to fend off the takeover
   C. Excessive use of debt

V. Leveraged Buyouts

VI. Bankruptcy and Reorganization
   A. Causes of business failure
   B. Voluntary reorganizations
   C. The order of claims
   D. Voluntary and involuntary bankruptcies

VII. Prepackaged Bankruptcies

VIII. Predicting Corporate Bankruptcy

SUMMARY

Many firms expand through external growth. They acquire or merge with other firms. There are three basic types of mergers. Horizontal mergers combine two companies in the same industry; vertical mergers combine a firm with its suppliers or distributors. Conglomerate mergers combine firms in different industries; the resulting firm has a diversified (and even unrelated) product line.

A merger may increase the earnings per share of the surviving firm. Even if earnings per share are initially decreased, the firm may be able to grow more rapidly. This is particularly true if synergy exists in which the surviving firm is stronger than the two firms were operating independently of each other.

Mergers are accounted for either by a pooling of interest or by the purchase method of accounting. Pooling is accomplished through a horizontal summation of the firms' balance sheets. Pooling is only permitted when specific conditions are met. With the purchase method of accounting, one firm is designated to have purchased the other firm. If the price paid exceeds the acquired firm's net worth, goodwill is created. Goodwill is amortized, which decreases the firm's earnings but, in this case, does not decrease taxes.

Mergers may be paid for with cash, with debt, or with stock. For stockholders of the acquired company, a stock swap offers maximum tax advantage. Such exchanges of like securities (that is the stock in the acquired firm is swapped for stock in the acquiring firm) are treated by the Internal Revenue Service as tax free exchanges. Acquisition effectuated through a swapping of stock for debt securities or a swapping of stock for cash are considered sales and are subject to appropriate capital gains taxation.

Not all business combinations are friendly. A firm may seek to acquire another and the management of the latter resists. In some cases, management finds a friendly buyer, or white knight, to purchase the firm and thus avoid the hostile takeover. In other cases, management takes actions such as selling off a division or significantly increasing the firm's outstanding debt. These actions are designed to discourage the takeover and maintain the independence of the firm and its management.

Instead of merging with another firm, some firms are sold to their managements. These individuals borrow the funds by pledging the assets of the corporation to secure the loans. The borrowed funds are then used to buy out the public stockholders. Such acquisitions of firms are called leveraged buyouts.

Financial mismanagement is a chief cause of insolvency and bankruptcy. A firm becomes insolvent when it is unable to meet its obligations as they come due. Voluntary restructuring of the agreements between the firm and its creditors may result. If the creditors are unwilling to accept such restructuring, they may force the firm into bankruptcy court in an effort to force payment. In other cases the insolvent firm may voluntarily seek protection from its creditors through bankruptcy proceedings.

In bankruptcy there is a specified order in which obligations are met. Court costs, wages, and taxes precede the claims of the secured and unsecured creditors. Secured creditors are paid initially from the proceeds of the sales of the collateral securing the loans. If such sales do not satisfy these claims, the secured creditors become general creditors.

Stockholders (preferred and common) have the last claim on the firm's assets. In many cases the unsecured and general creditors are willing to accept a reorganization instead of a liquidation, since sales of assets rarely will raise sufficient funds to compensate these creditors in full. In some cases the firm may work out a reorganization plan prior to a bankruptcy filing in order to facilitate the process.

FILL IN THE BLANKS

1. If a merger causes two weak firms to prosper, it may be the result of _____.

2. Mergers may be classified as _____, _____, and _____.

3. The advantage of swapping stock instead of accepting cash in a merger is _____.

4. If the purchase price of the firm acquired through a merger exceeds the firm's net worth, _____ will be created.

5. The merger of Dow Chemical and Allied Chemical would be an example of a _____ merger.

6. The purchase of a firm by management through the use of debt which may be secured by the firm's assets is a _____.

7. An attempted takeover of a firm may be thwarted if management is able to sell the firm for a higher price to a _____.

8. Bankruptcy proceedings tend to stress the _____ of the firm.

9. In a liquidation, accrued wages owed and taxes are paid _____ general creditors.

10. In a reorganization the old general creditors often become the _____ of the reorganized firm.

11. A reorganization plan that is worked prior to filing for bankruptcy is called a _____.

12. Excess use of _____ is often a cause of business failure.

PROBLEMS

1. Two firms with the following balance sheets merge. Construct the new balance sheet if the merger is treated as a pooling of interest.

Firm A Balance Sheet as of 1/31/XX

Assets		Liabilities and Equity	
Accounts receivable	$2,000	Accounts payable	$1,000
Inventory	3,000	Mortgage loan	4,000
Land	1,000		
Plant	5,000	Equity	8,000
Investments	2,000		
	$13,000		$13,000

Firm B Balance Sheet as of 1/31/XX

Assets		Liabilities and Equity	
Cash	$1,000	Short-term notes	$3,000
Accounts receivable	3,000	Long-term debt	5,000
Inventory	7,000		
Plant	9,000	Equity	12,000
	$20,000		$20,000

2. What will be the earnings per share of the combined firm if Firm A swaps 1.2 shares of its stock for 1.0 shares of Firm B's stock?

	Firm A	Firm B
Earnings per share	$2.00	$1.30
Number of shares outstanding	10,000	7,000
Growth rate	10%	14%

If the price/earnings ratio of Firm A before the merger was 10.0 and does not change, what will be the price of Firm A's stock after the merger? What would be expected to happen to Firm A's growth rate in the future?

TRUE/FALSE

T F 1. A merger of two firms in the same industry is an example of a conglomerate merger.

T F 2. A merger between a firm and one of its suppliers is a vertical merger.

T F 3. A firm that produces varied products like liquor, chemicals, and metals may be classified as a conglomerate.

T F 4. When two firms merge, earnings per share increase if the merger is treating as a pooling of interests.

T F 5. A merger may be accomplished by swapping new debt for stock.

T F 6. A cash purchase of a firm and a resulting merger is exempt from capital gains taxes.

T F 7. One advantage of the hostile takeover is that involuntary gains generated by the sale of the stock are not subject to federal taxation.

T F 8. If a firm buys a company for stock, the resulting merger is exempt from federal income taxation.

T F 9. If a firm issues debt to execute a merger, its use of financial leverage is increased.

T F 10. Goodwill arises when one firm pays more for the assets of another firm than the assets' book value.

T F 11. When goodwill is amortized, it reduces the firm's taxes.

T F 12. If management buys out the public stockholders by issuing debt secured by the firm's assets, that is a leveraged buyout.

T F 13. If a firm defaults on its debt obligations, creditors may seek payment through a court proceeding.

T F 14. A firm may default on a loan even if it makes the interest payments.

T F 15. A firm cannot voluntarily seek court protection from its creditors.

T F 16. If a bankrupt firm is liquidated, secured creditors are paid from the general funds of the firm.

T F 17. In a reorganization the old creditors may become the new stockholders of the new firm.

T F 18. The emphasis in bankruptcy court is on liquidating the firm.

T F 19. In a liquidation, court costs are paid after secured claims.

T F 20. Unsecured creditors often prefer reorganization to liquidation.

T F 21. A firm and its creditors may not work out a plan of reorganization prior to filing for bankruptcy.

T F 22. A white knight is a firm that saves a failing firm from a bankruptcy filing.

T F 23. Leveraged buyouts may end in bankruptcy since the firms have insufficient equity financing.

MULTIPLE CHOICE

1. External growth is achieved through
   1. issuing new securities
   2. retaining earnings
   3. mergers
      a. 1 and 2
      b. 1 and 3
      c. 1, 2, and 3
      d. only 3

2. Mergers justified on the grounds that the combined firm is worth
   more than the two individual firms by themselves is called a
   a. synergistic merger
   b. vertical merger
   c. horizontal merger
   d. profitable merger

3. A merger effectuated by a swapping of stock offers stockholders
   which advantage?
   a. the swap is only subject to income tax
   b. the new shares will appreciate in value
   c. the swap is subject to capital gains tax instead of income tax
   d. any tax liability is deferred until the new shares are sold

4. If a merger is accounted for by the "purchase" method of
   accounting, goodwill
   a. can not occur
   b. occurs if the assets are worth more than the firm paid for
      them
   c. occurs if the assets are worth less than the firm paid for
      them
   d. occurs if the assets are worth less than the firm paid for
      them and the firm is unable to increase their value on its
      books

5. In pooling
   a. the assets of the two firms are combined
   b. the liabilities of the two firms are combined
   c. the assets and liabilities of the two firms are combined
   d. goodwill is created

6. Creditors may accept a voluntary reorganization because
   1. their loans lack collateral
   2. court proceedings are costly
   3. the reorganized firm has potential to succeed
      a. 1 and 2
      b. 1 and 3
      c. 2 and 3
      d. 1, 2, and 3

7. In a liquidation the order of payment is
   a. stockholders, creditors, court costs
   b. creditors, court costs, stockholders
   c. court costs, stockholders, creditors
   d. court costs, creditors, stockholders

8. One defense used by management to thwart an unwanted takeover is
   a. the use of pooling
   b. a leveraged buyout
   c. a bankruptcy proceeding
   d. hoarding cash

9. A leveraged buyout may lead to bankruptcy because
   a. the firm uses too much equity financing
   b. goodwill decreases the firm's earnings
   c. the firm uses excess debt financing
   d. operating income declines because of the additional interest

10. In a prepackaged bankruptcy
    a. the court works out a plan of reorganization
    b. the stockholders give their shares to the firm's creditors
    c. management and creditors work out a reorganization plan
    d. a reorganization plan is established prior to bankruptcy

11. Which of the following may indicate a firm's financial position
    is declining?
    a. the debt ratio and times-interest-earned are increasing
    b. the debt ratio and times-interest earned are decreasing
    c. the debt ratio is increasing and times-interest-earned is
       decreasing
    d. the debt ratio is decreasing and times-interest-earned is
       increasing

ANSWERS TO FILL IN THE BLANKS

1. synergy
2. horizontal, vertical, conglomerate
3. the transaction is not considered a realized
   sale by the IRS (therefore, no tax)
4. goodwill
5. horizontal
6. leveraged buyout
7. white knight
8. reorganization
9. before
10. stockholders
11. prepackaged bankruptcy
12. financial leverage

ANSWERS TO PROBLEMS

1.

Firm AB Combined Balance Sheets as of 1/31/XX

Assets		Liabilities and Equity	
Cash	$1,000	Trade accounts	$1,000
Accounts receivable	5,000	Short-term notes	3,000
Inventory	10,000	Mortgage loan	4,000
Plant	14,000	Long-term debt	5,000
Land	1,000		
Investments	2,000	Equity	20,000
	$33,000		$33,000

All that has occurred is a horizontal summation of all the accounts. Even if the value of the stock swapped as part of the merger exceeds the value of the acquired assets, goodwill does not arise.

2. Determination of new earnings per share:

Total earnings: $2.00 x 10,000 + $1.30 x 7,000 = $29,100

Number of shares: 10,000 + 1.2(7,000) = 18,400

Earnings per share: $29,100/18,400 = $1.58

Value of the stock if the P/E ratio remains 10:
  10 x $1.58 = $15.80

The price of the stock declines from $20 to $15.80. Obviously this is not desirable unless the firm's future growth is enhanced by the merger so that the value will rise more rapidly in the future. However, the decline in the price of the stock indicates that the security market does not believe that such rapid growth will occur.

Chapter 25
OVERVIEW OF CORPORATE FINANCIAL MANAGEMENT

I. The Role of the Financial Manager
   A. Liquidity versus profitability
   B. Capital budgeting
   C. Optimal capital structure
   D. Matching assets and their sources of finance

II. The Impact of Competition
   A. Competition for
      1. Markets
      2. Sources of finance
   B. Foreign competition

III. The Impact of Fiscal and Monetary Policy on Financial Decision Making
   A. Monetary policy and the ability of the banking system to create money and credit
   B. The ability of the financial manager to anticipate changes in monetary and fiscal policy

IV. The Purpose of the Book Restated
   A. Finance: a crucial component of business
   B. Finance: an inescapable part of life

SUMMARY

The role of the financial manager is many-faceted. The job encompasses (1) planning and forecasting, (2) selecting among competing investment alternatives, (3) analyzing financial statements, and (4) deciding the amount of financial leverage the firm should use.

The criterion by which performance is judged is value. The financial manager should take those actions which increase the value of the firm.

The financial manager's job is difficult because the firm does not operate in a vacuum. The firm faces competition from domestic and foreign firms for its markets and its sources of finance. In addition, national economic goals and the means to achieve these goals affect the firm. The financial manager cannot ignore the monetary policy of the Federal Reserve or the fiscal policy of the federal government.

Successful business requires successful financial management. Poor financial management is a prime cause of business failure. Knowledge of financial institutions and the tools of financial management is a first step toward successful financial management.

Finance is also an inescapable part of modern life. Individuals must also make financial decisions. Thus many of the principals and institutional settings also apply to personal financial management.

TRUE/FALSE

T F 1. The financial manager's job includes planning and forecasting.

T F 2. The optimal capital structure is concerned with obtaining the advantages of financial leverage without unduly increasing risk.

T F 3. Liquidity versus profitability refers to a firm's having sufficient investments to earn interest.

T F 4. A financial manager should match the type of financing with the asset being financed.

T F 5. Commercial banks are a major source of short-term finance.

T F 6. Commercial banks' capacity to lend depends on their excess reserves.

T F 7. Commercial banks' ability to lend is increased by transactions on the New York Stock Exchange.

T F 8. The ultimate control of the money supply rests with the U. S. Treasury.

T F 9. How the federal government's deficit is financed can have no impact on the supply of money and credit.

T F 10. The nation's central bank is the Federal Reserve, and it seeks to control the nation's supply of money.

T F 11. Capital budgeting refers to making long-term investments in plant and equipment.

T F 12. Financial risk refers to the risk associated with the firm's use of financial leverage.

T F 13. Liquidity refers to the ease of converting an asset into cash without a loss.

T F 14. The goals of economic policy include stable prices, increased unemployment, and economic growth.

T F 15. Foreign competition applies to a domestic firm's markets but not its sources of finance.

MULTIPLE CHOICE

1. The financial manager's job includes
    1. analysis of financial statements
    2. determining the firm's optimal capital structure
    3. capital budgeting decisions
        a. 1 and 2
        b. 1 and 3
        c. 2 and 3
        d. 1, 2, and 3

2. Long-term sources of finance include
    a. trade credit and bonds
    b. accounts payable and debentures
    c. mortgages and debentures
    d. common stock and trade credit

3. Short-term sources of funds include
    a. debentures and bank loans
    b. commercial paper and bank loans
    c. preferred stock and factoring
    d. trade credit and accounts receivable

4. Excess cash may be temporarily invested in
    1. Treasury bills
    2. debentures
    3. commercial paper
        a. 1 and 2
        b. 1 and 3
        c. 2 and 3
        d. 1, 2, and 3

5. Financial risk refers to
    a. the nature of the business
    b. the firm's sources of funds
    c. the quality of the financial manager
    d. the maximization of value

6. Business risk refers to
    a. the nature of the business
    b. the firm's sources of funds
    c. the quality of the financial manager
    d. the maximization of value

7. The supply of money is controlled by
    a. commercial banks
    b. the U. S. Treasury
    c. the Federal Reserve
    d. the Securities and Exchange Commission

8. The capacity of banks to lend depends on
   1. their total reserves
   2. the reserve requirements
   3. the public's willingness to deposit funds in commercial banks
      a. 1 and 2
      b. 1 and 3
      c. 2 and 3
      d. 1, 2, and 3

9. Transactions that affect the reserves of commercial banks include
   1. lending funds directly to a corporation by buying a new issue of bonds
   2. depositing cash in a savings account
   3. the Federal Reserve's purchasing bonds
      a. 1 and 2
      b. 1 and 3
      c. 2 and 3
      d. 1, 2, and 3

10. The purposes of monetary policy include
    1. increasing employment
    2. stimulating economic growth
    3. stabilizing prices
       a. 1 and 2
       b. 1 and 3
       c. 2 and 3
       d. 1, 2, and 3

11. Monetary and fiscal policy affect the firm by
    1. altering the cost of capital
    2. altering the demand for the firm's products
    3. changing the tax and regulatory environment
       a. 1 and 2
       b. 1 and 3
       c. 2 and 3
       d. 1, 2, and 3

12. Foreign competition affects
    a. monetary policy
    b. fiscal policy
    c. a firm's sources of finance
    d. open market operations

13. The criterion by which the financial manager is judged is the maximization of
    a. profits
    b. sales
    c. salaries
    d. value

ANSWERS TO TRUE/FALSE

Chapter: Question:	1	2	3	4	5	6	7	8	9	10	11	12	13	14	15	16	17	18
1	F	F	F	F	F	F	T	F	F	T	F	T	F	F	F	T	F	F
2	T	F	F	T	T	T	F	T	F	F	F	F	F	T	F	T	T	T
3	F	F	F	F	T	F	F	T	T	T	T	T	F	F	T	F	T	T
4	F	T	F	F	F	F	T	F	T	T	F	F	T	T	T	F	F	F
5	F	T	F	F	T	T	F	T	F	T	T	T	F	T	T	F	F	F
6	F	F	F	F	F	T	F	F	F	F	T	T	T	F	T	F	T	F
7	T	T	F	T	T	T	T	T	F	T	T	F	T	F	F	T	F	T
8	T	F	T	F	F	T	F	F	F	T	T	F	F	T	T	F	T	F
9	T	T	F	T	T	T	F	T	F	T	F	T	F	T	T	T	F	T
10	T	T	F	T	F	F	T	F	F	T	F	F	T	T	F	F	T	F
11		F	T	F	F	T	T	T	T	F	F	F	T	T	F	F	T	F
12		F	F	T	F	T	F	F	T	T	T	F	F	F	F	F	T	F
13		F	F	T	T	T	T	T	T	T	F	F	F	F	F	F	T	F
14		F	T	T	T	F	F	T	T	T	T		T		T	T	T	T
15		F	F	T	F	T	T	T	F	F			T		T	T	T	F
16		T	F	T	T	T	T	T	F	F			T		F	T	T	
17		T	T	T	T	T	F	T	T	T			T		F	F	T	
18		T	T	F					F	F			T		F	F	T	
19		T	T	T					T	F			T		T	F	T	
20		F	F	T					F	F			T		T	T	F	
21		F		F									F		T	T	F	
22				T									T		F	T	F	
23													T		F	F	F	
24													T		F	T	T	
25													T			F		
26													F			T		
27													T			T		
28													T			F		
29													F			F		
30													T			T		
31																T		
32																F		
33																F		
34																T		
35																F		
36																F		
37																F		
38																F		
39																T		
40																T		
41																		

Chapter:	19	20	21	22	23	24	25
Question:							
1	T	F	F	F	F	F	T
2	F	F	T	T	T	T	T
3	T	T	F	F	T	T	F
4	T	T	F	T	F	F	T
5	T	F	T	T	F	T	T
6	T	T	F	T	F	F	T
7	F	T	T	T	T	F	F
8	T	T	F	F	F	T	F
9	F	F	F	T	T	T	F
10	F	T	F	T	F	T	T
11	T	T	T	F	T	F	T
12	F	F	T	T	T	T	T
13	F	F	T	T	T	T	T
14	T	T	F	F	T	T	F
15	F	F		F	T	F	F
16	T	T		F	T	F	
17	F	T		T	F	T	
18	F	F		T	T	F	
19	T	T			F	F	
20	T	T			F	T	
21	F	F				T	
22	T	T				F	
23	F					T	
24	T						
25	T						
26	F						
27	F						
28	F						

ANSWERS TO MULTIPLE CHOICE

Chapter:	1	2	3	4	5	6	7	8	9	10	11	12	13	14	15	16	17	18
Question:																		
1	d	b	b	a	b	d	d	d	a	d	d	c	c	d	a	b	a	c
2	d	b	c	b	b	b	d	a	b	a	d	b	a	c	a	d	d	b
3	b	c	d	d	a	b	b	a	d	d	b	c	b	b	b	c	d	b
4	c	c	c	b	b	d	b	c	b	a	c	c	b	d	c	c	b	c
5	c	c	a	a	a	d	c	c	c	a	b	b	d	d	c	c	d	a
6	b	a	c	b	b	a	d	b	b	c	b	b	a	d	c	c	d	d
7	c	a	c	d	d	d	d	c	a	a	d	c	b	c	d	d	d	b
8		d	c	d	a	c	a	a	d	a			d	a	a	b	a	b
9		c	d	c	b	d	b	c	d	d			b	b	c	b	d	a
10		c	b	a		a	b	a	d	a			c	c	b	a	d	b
11		b	c	a		c	b		d	a			d	d		b	a	
12			d	b		d	a		d				b			c	a	
13				a		d			d				d			b	b	
14				a									b			c	b	
15				b												c		
16				a												c		
17				c												a		
18				a												c		
19				b												a		
20				d												a		
21				c														
22				b														
23				b														

Chapter:	19	20	21	22	23	24	25
Question:							
1	d	c	b	a	b	b	d
2	d	c	a	b	c	a	c
3	b	a	b	b	d	d	b
4	c	d	d	d	c	d	b
5	b	b	d	d	c	c	b
6	c	b	a	c	d	d	a
7	c	b	b	a	b	d	c
8	d	a	b	d	b	b	d
9	a	a	d	d	a	c	c
10	b	b	d	b	d	d	d
11	b	d	d	c	d	c	d
12	d			a			c
13	a			d			d
14	c			d			
15	c			b			
16	a						
17	c						